THE
WILD BOY
OF
BURUNDI

HARLAN LANE & RICHARD PILLARD

THE
WILD BOY
OF
BURUNDI

A STUDY OF AN OUTCAST CHILD

RANDOM HOUSE NEW YORK

Excerpt from the article written by Görel Day-Wilson for *Kvällsposten*
of Malmö, Sweden. Reprinted by permission.
Excerpt from the letter to *The New York Times* by Jeff Lang, September 6,
1972, © 1972 by The New York Times Company. Reprinted by permission.
Cartoon by Reiser reprinted by permission of *Charlie Hebdo,* Paris.

Library of Congress Cataloging in Publication Data

Lane, Harlan L
The Wild Boy of Burundi.

1. Autism—Cases, clinical reports, statistics.
2. Wild Boy of Burundi.   I. Pillard, Richard,
joint author.
RJ506.A9L36   618.9′28′98209   77–90316
ISBN 0–394–41252–4

Manufactured in the United States of America
2 4 6 8 9 7 5 3
First Edition

BURUNDI

—————————— 40 mls

Rwanda

Murore

MUYINGA

Muyinga

Cibitoke • Ibuye
Bubanza • Ngozi

BUBANZA NGOZI Muramba • Mugera

Kigamba

Muzinda

Kayongozi

Muramvya RUYIGI

BUJUMBURA Gitega Ruyigi

Zaïre MURAMVYA GITEGA

Matana

Rumonge BURURI

Bururi

Tanzania

Bukemba

Nyanza-Lac

Lake
Tanganyika

Buzizi R.

Ruvuvu R.

Malagarasi R.

Kagera R.

THOMAS BRENNAN

FOR FRANK AND DAVID

*Il y a toujours plus tard des savants qui s'occupent de ça, pour
essayer d'expliquer
comment c'est arrivé.*

—Emile Ajar,
Gros-Câlin

ACKNOWLEDGMENTS

We gratefully acknowledge the contributions of the following individuals who were critical to the success of our mission in Burundi. *In the United States:* Mr. David Cardwell, Burundi desk officer, U.S. State Department; Dr. Lewis Lipsitt, Brown University; Dr. Peter Marler, Rockefeller University; Ms. Mary McKay, Northeastern University Press Bureau; Dr. Martin Moore-Ede, Harvard University School of Medicine; Mr. Vincent Ollivier, Northeastern University; Dr. Peter Rosenberger, Massachusetts General Hospital; Dr. Clement Sambira, chargé d'affaires, Republic of Burundi; Dr. Philip Sapir, director, William T. Grant Foundation; Mr. Benn Shedd, producer, *Nova;* Dr. Alex Skavenski, Northeastern University; Dr. B. F. Skinner, Harvard University; Rev. Paul Sorelle, provincial, White Fathers; Mr. Thomas Sprague, Northeastern University Press Bureau; Dr. Laurence Stoddard, Northeastern University; Dr. Michael Terman, Northeastern University; Dr. Frank R. Wilson, San Francisco. *In Burundi:* Dr.

ACKNOWLEDGMENTS

Deogratias Barakamfitiye, director of medical training, Province of Gitega; Prof. Cyrille Barancira, University of Burundi; Dr. Frederico Bartoli, World Health Organization; Mr. Septime Bizimana, governor, Province of Gitega; Dr. Paul Ghipponi, director, Forami Laboratories; Ms. Harriet Isom, deputy chief of mission, U.S. Embassy, Bujumbura; Fr. Juvenal Kadogo, vicar, Archdiocese of Gitega; Mr. David Kaeuper, economic attaché, U.S. Embassy, Bujumbura; Msgr. André Makarakiza, archbishop of Gitega; Mr. David Mark, ambassador of the United States to the Republic of Burundi; Mme. Imelda Ndikumana, supervisor, Orphélinat de Bujumbura; Nicéphore Ndimurukundi, University of Burundi; Dr. Joseph Nindorera, minister of public health; Sr. Nestor Nzisabira, directress, Orphélinat de la Providence, Gitega; Fr. Claude Pagé, White Fathers, Bujumbura; Diane Shelly Panasik, University of Burundi; Sr. Tonia Roelens, I.C.M., Bujumbura; Petronille Sinibarura, aide, Orphélinat de la Providence, Gitega; Fr. Pierre Tuhabonye, treasurer, Archdiocese of Gitega; Sr. Marie-Jeanne Verhoeven, I.C.M., Munanira; Dr. Viatcheslav Zarotchintsev, psychiatrist, Prince Regent Charles Hospital. *In Kenya:* Mr. Arcade Bankamwabo, Burundi consul in Nairobi; Dr. Alan Cross, pediatrician, Kenyatta Hospital; Mr. Titus Muoka, Kenyatta Hospital; Dr. Martin Oduori, senior government pediatrician, Kenyatta Hospital; Dr. J. J. Thuku, chief administrator, Kenyatta Hospital.

This book would not have been written without the support of the William T. Grant Foundation and the encouragement of Jason Epstein and Gail Winston of Random House. Several colleagues read the manuscript and made helpful suggestions: Robbin Battison, Michael Callen, François Grosjean, Nicholas Morris, Franklin Philip, and David Steiger. The tales of a missionary's life in Burundi, attributed here to a Fr. Masseroni, were actually taken from a book by Fr. D. Carlo Masseroni, *Urakoze Dawe!* Paolo Zacchera called the book to our attention, and David Steiger prepared translations from the original Italian. It is a pleasure to acknowledge, too, the skillful typing of Marla Richmond and Geni Donaghey.

The following articles and books were particularly helpful in preparing our manuscript, and we are pleased to note them here. E. Albert,

ACKNOWLEDGMENTS

"Culture Patterning of Speech Behavior in Burundi," in J. Gumperz and D. Hymes, eds., *Directions in Sociolinguistics* (New York: Holt, Rinehart & Winston, 1972); M. Bowen, G. Freeman, and K. Miller, *Passing By: The United States and Genocide in Burundi, 1972* (New York: Carnegie Endowment for International Peace, 1972); S. Curtiss, *Genie: A Psycholinguistic Study of a Modern-day "Wild Child"* (New York: Academic Press, 1977); *Johannesburg Times,* April 11, 1976; *Kvällsposten,* December 25, 1975; H. Lane, *The Wild Boy of Aveyron* (Cambridge, Mass.: Harvard University Press, 1976); R. Lemarchand, *Rwanda and Burundi* (New York: Praeger, 1970); G. C. McDonald, ed., *Area Handbook for Burundi* (Washington, D.C.: U.S. Government Printing Office, 1969); T. P. Melady, *Burundi: The Tragic Years* (New York: Orbis, 1974); J. R. Napier and P. H. Napier, *A Handbook of Living Primates* (New York: Academic Press, 1967); E. M. Ornitz and E. R. Ritvo, "The Syndrome of Autism: A Critical Review," *American Journal of Psychiatry,* June 1976; C. Rabeyrin, *Mgr. F. Gerboin, 1847–1912* (Langeac: Mont Sainte Catherine, 1973); E. R. Ritvo, ed., *Autism: Diagnosis, Current Research and Management* (New York: Spectrum, 1976); F. Tinland, *L'Homme Sauvage* (Paris: Payot, 1968); L. Wing, *Early Childhood Autism* (New York: Pergamon, 1976).

FOREWORD

When I received a report that a boy had been found running with a troupe of monkeys in a small country in Africa, I naturally turned to Harlan Lane. In *The Wild Boy of Aveyron* (1976), Lane tells the well-documented story of Victor, a feral boy of the early nineteenth century who was never fully restored to society in spite of the heroic and imaginative efforts of his teacher, Jean-Marc Itard—efforts which nevertheless influenced the instruction of young children throughout the nineteenth century. Lane conducted his research on Victor's story in the Bibliothèque Nationale and other archives in Paris. The place which he and his colleague, Richard Pillard, reconstructed the story of John, the wild boy of Burundi, was very different. Burundi is possibly the poorest, unhealthiest, and politically least stable country in the world. If the boy was truly feral, it would be necessary to move quickly "before civilization set in," and the account of how the authors got financial support, visas, permission, inoculations, supplies, and transportation under pressure of time is absorbing. (Lane had the advantage of speaking French, which is the main Western language in Burundi.)

In one scene in the book, a Burundian watches his portrait slowly appear in a Polariod snapshot. "Is it magic?" he asks. Many readers will experience a sense of magic as they watch the true story of the wild boy unfold—but not because they will find him in any part of their own image. Lane and Pillard argue that we are fascinated by Tarzan, Robinson Crusoe, and Mowgli (and they should not forget Rima and her green mansions) because we long to be free of the restraints of civilization. But they rightly point out that few of us would forgo the pleasures and advantages of civilization, and certainly no one would want to be the wild boy of Burundi.

The account is, I think, fascinating for a different reason. It has the archetypal pattern of the search for a person—for an "identity." It is a problem familiar to all psychiatrists. Patients are not hard to find; indeed, they seek out psychiatrists. But the real search has only then just begun. The wild boy was not hard to find, either, but where were Lane and Pillard to find the explanation of his bizarre behavior, his strange utterances?

The notion of an identity is troublesome. The answer was to be found not within the boy himself but in his history—in the conditions which had converted a living body into a strange person. There were two possibilities, as there are for the psychiatrists. The critical condition might be biological—an inherited defect, a childhood disease—or it might be environmental—in particular, the rare condition of a world stripped of human contact.

I doubt whether a psychiatrist ever worked under more difficult conditions or at greater risk to discover the key to a personal problem. Certainly, few ever reach a more satisfactory resolution.

—B. F. Skinner

CONTENTS

THE
WILD BOY
OF
BURUNDI

I

A WILD BOY
IS FOUND

Deep in the dense tropical forest of Burundi in Central Africa, a band
of soldiers picked their way cautiously through tangled undergrowth. The
date was June 2, 1974, and the soldiers were patrolling an isolated area
in south Burundi, far from the nearest settlement.

Suddenly a troop of grey enkende monkeys caught sight of the men,
and screaming warnings to their companions, they scattered to the tops
of nearby trees, chattering and swaying on the highest branches.

The soldiers paid little attention, monkeys are common in that part
of the forest.

Then one of the soldiers noted something odd. One monkey was still
struggling up a tree, displaying far less agility than his companions.

The soldier peered into the dim light which filtered through the
trees, and what he saw caused him to yell to his companions and rub his
eyes in disbelief.

There, naked and chattering in anger, climbing as fast as he could,
was a little human boy. The Burundi soldier had stumbled upon some-

thing of which men have only dreamed—a real live jungle boy, a miniature Tarzan, a boy who lived with a troop of monkeys and was accepted as one of the tribe.

When I read these opening lines a few weeks after they appeared in the *Johannesburg Sunday Times* for April 11, 1976, I had ample reason for disbelief. First, the story smacked of sensationalism: it was a full-page spread under the blazing banner THE BOY WHO THINKS HE'S A MONKEY, and it had a full-color picture of a black boy, wearing only a breechcloth, seated in a grassy field in front of a bowl; he was shown fanning his face, his splayed fingers covered with banana mash. The caption read: "Out of the wilderness . . . John the Jungle Boy, named after John the Baptist."

Then, too, I had never heard of Burundi, and even if there was such a place (which was likely, after all), a dense tropical forest in a remote African nation was just too pat a setting—the sort of place you would expect to find John the Jungle Boy, and also Tarzan, Mowgli, and other wild men who inhabit man's mind but not his planet.

But the main reason for my skepticism was that I dared not believe my good fortune if the story was true. The last time a child had been found who was unquestionably feral—that is, raised in the wilderness without human contact—was almost two centuries ago, in 1799. The boy had clambered out of the forests in southern France, worked his way across an elevated plateau during the bitter winter months, and entered a farmhouse on the edge of a hamlet. There he exchanged the freedom and isolation of his life in the forests of Aveyron, where he had run wild, for captivity and the company of men in society. He came without a name, so he was called the Wild Boy of Aveyron. Even though that boy had appeared at the dawn of psychology and psychiatry, when no one knew how to study a deviant child, much less treat one, mankind had reaped immeasurable benefits from his capture. Modern methods for educating the deaf, the retarded, and the normal preschool child arose directly out of the efforts to train him.

The wild boy's teacher, a twenty-six-year-old physician from the provinces named Jean-Marc Gaspard Itard, set out to train this *enfant sauvage;* by his labor's end, he had become the originator of instructional devices, the inventor of what we now call behavior modification, and the father of special education for the mentally and physically handicapped. Itard's approach to rehabilitation—education of the senses—gained breadth and momentum in the hands of his student, Edward Seguin, who went on to establish the education of the retarded when this was universally believed impossible. As he witnessed retarded children throughout the world benefit from his labors, Seguin, in his later years, foresaw how the lessons learned in the education of the handicapped could revolutionize the education of all children. Maria Montessori fulfilled that vision in the twentieth century as Seguin had fulfilled Itard's in the nineteenth: she extended Itard's program for the wild boy first to the early stages of child development, before formal education, and then to all of education, whatever the age of the learner, revising our concept of education itself. Montessori died only a few decades ago. But our society has so thoroughly absorbed what this evolving system of education offered that we barely recognize its various features, understand why they were sensational discoveries at the time, or appreciate the struggle and the vision of those who rode the stream of history and also changed its course, from Itard and the Wild Boy to Montessori and the Children's Houses.

Suppose another wild boy were now granted us, in the middle of the twentieth century. How much more could we now learn with the tools of modern psychology and medicine! How much more could we discover about what it means to grow up in society from this terrible experiment of nature, which chance had designed and which science could exploit? And how much more could we contribute to the education of handicapped children everywhere by undertaking the training of this latest, and perhaps last, wild child, raised in the forests utterly cut off from society?

The nineteenth century asked of the Wild Boy of Aveyron: What makes us human? Is it that we walk upright (but you run on all fours)? Is it that we have language (but you are mute)? Are there ideas without language (what are yours)? Are the tender emotions learned (do you know how to love)? Does all knowledge really come from the senses

THE WILD BOY OF BURUNDI

(what do you know that was not in your experience)? The twentieth century would ask of John, the Jungle Boy of Burundi: How do man's senses change to adapt to life in the wild? Which of our discriminations, perceptions, and motives, on the other hand, require growing up in human society? Is the human endowment for language learning so nonspecific that a child reared by monkeys will learn their system of vocal communication? Indeed, will one primate species actually rear a child from another? Can modern methods of behavior modification rehabilitate a child reared outside of human society—even teach him language? If John was really a monkey boy, he would be able to answer questions such as these, and many more.

I had another reason, a more personal one, for a keen interest in John. A few weeks before John the Jungle Boy appeared on the feature page of the *Johannesburg Times,* my book on the Wild Boy of Aveyron had appeared in the bookstores. Victor, as he was christened on his return to society in 1800, had been my constant companion, in a manner of speaking, for two years. After spending countless hours in archives, libraries, and storage rooms, after searching in Paris and in the provinces, after studying manuscripts, letters, newspaper articles, and books, I knew as much about Victor as any man had ever known: the number of scars on his body and where they were; his peculiar tastes in food; where he kept each thing in his room. I could see his rocking gait and his wandering gaze, I could hear his inarticulate cries and feel his yearning to be free again in the forests. I truly felt like the philosopher who said about Victor: "I would rather spend one hour with this boy than one week with the finest minds in Europe." And now I might be granted this impossible wish. I would get to know a live wild boy, John of Burundi. I couldn't believe it. It was too good to be true. Of course, it might not be true. But one had to find out. It was like Pascal's wager: however small the odds that there is a god, the reward of eternal salvation is worth no end of religious devotion.

I am not in the habit of reading the *Johannesburg Times.* I get my diet of human tragedy from the *Boston Globe,* my scientific discoveries from a few professional journals, and my ration of myth from interoffice memos. Harvard psychology professor B. F. Skinner sent me the news clipping about John the Jungle Boy along with a letter he had

received from the son of the Peace Corps director in Botswana. It was
dated just five days earlier, April 14, 1976. The letter read:

Dear Dr. Skinner:
    The enclosed article appeared in the *Johannesburg Sunday Times*.
After reading of the treatment (type and quality) the boy was getting, I
immediately thought of the behaviorist practitioners as the people most
able to resolve responsibly the conflict between the need to learn and the
respect and loving willingness to help due this so vulnerable person.
    Please give this serious attention: the people "treating" him now
could break him or kill him *if he doesn't get away.*
    I would be more than willing to give you any assistance I can if you
decide to take some action.
    Thank you.

                                            Charles Taylor

    When Skinner had called me the day before, I thought it was to
thank me for sending him a dedicated copy of my book; he had directed
my doctoral thesis, and in any case, no psychologist could work on
human learning without building on the foundations B. F. Skinner had
laid.
    "Harlan, Fred Skinner. They've found another wild boy, in
Africa."
    "I beg your pardon."
    "Another Victor. When could you leave?"
    "Where is he?"
    "In Burundi. I'll send you the newspaper article."
    "Well, there's the problem of verifying the story. And finding the
money to go."
    "Yes."
    "And finding Burundi."
    "This could be a very important discovery. See what you think
when you read the story."

    "The story of John the Jungle Boy is one of the strangest ever
written," the newspaper article continued. I had to agree.

‡ 8 ‡

THE WILD BOY OF BURUNDI

STORY

John is now about eight years old. It is believed that when he was four, he was abruptly orphaned and left alone in the heart of the African bush. By a million-to-one chance, he was discovered by a tribe of monkeys who adopted and cared for him.

Until he was rescued by soldiers two years later, he lived the life of a monkey in the Burundi forest.

Today in spite of painstaking attempts to "rehabilitate" him, he remains to all intents and purposes a monkey. He is unable to talk and communicates by "monkey" grunts and chattering. He will eat only fruit and vegetables, and when excited or scared jumps up and down uttering threatening monkey cries.

A Russian psychiatrist has taught him to walk upright—when rescued he could only scramble along on all fours. The psychiatrist says there is "no hope of rehabilitating him further."

PRIEST

Father Pierre Tuhabonye, the Catholic priest in charge of the orphanage where the boy is now living, told me it's a miracle he survived at all.

"We named him John after John the Baptist because he too spent a long time in the wilderness."

John's story starts in 1972. A vicious civil war was raging between the Tutsi and Hutu tribes which share Burundi. It was a bloody war with no quarter given on either side.

The Tutsi emerged victorious and were merciless to the people who had opposed them. They systematically exterminated entire Hutu villages, particularly in the south of the country where the war began.

A Catholic priest who lives in the area where John was found told me: "No one can be certain how it happened that John was left alone. Most likely his parents were killed by Tutsi soldiers and he ran into the forest. By a million-to-one chance he was discovered by the monkeys who adopted him."

PROBLEM

"John's discovery created a problem for the Burundi government. He was a reminder of an era in their history which they are trying hard to pretend never happened.

A WILD BOY IS FOUND

"To avoid an unpleasant investigation they packed him off to an orphanage with as little publicity as possible."

(Now that the story has been out for several weeks, I wonder how the Burundi government is handling the publicity. Are newsmen swarming over the orphanage? Has the boy been moved again, perhaps placed out of reach of all foreigners?)

The soldiers who discovered John returned hotfoot to their post in Nyanza Lac on the shores of Lake Tanganyika. From Nyanza Lac the boy was taken to Burundi's capital, Bujumbura, and placed in the town's only orphanage, the Orphélinat Officiel de Bujumbura.

"He was simply an animal when he arrived," said Mrs. Imelda Ndikumana, who is in charge of the orphanage. "We could do nothing with him. He walked on all fours, could not chew food and made monkey noises.

"He was terrified of other children and had no idea what a bed was. He refused to be put in a cot and instead slept curled up on the floor. He chattered constantly, and his first reaction when someone came near him was to try and climb up and away from them.

"There was nothing we could do with him or for him, and so we had no alternative but to send him to the Hospital of Prince Regent Charles in Bujumbura, where he was placed in a ward for the insane."

The hospital is large and understaffed. The ward for the insane is situated at the rear of the building and is separated from the rest of the hospital by a green wooden fence which reaches from floor to ceiling. An aide armed with a wooden stick sits at the fence 24 hours a day.

Inside the ward, patients dressed in gaily coloured robes favoured by many of the Burundi people sit in silence staring at points which only they can see. Others scream excitedly at the approach of visitors or tremble violently and creep away. This was John's home for 18 months.

Nurse Elizabeth Noigenegene is in charge of the ward. She is a small friendly person who tries hard to help her patients with the limited resources she has available.

"I knew the little boy from the day he arrived. I cared for him. There was no doubt that he considered himself a monkey, and he certainly behaved like one.

"He could not walk but scrambled along on all fours. He had thick calluses on his hands and knees, and he was covered with a fine coat of dark hair on his back and legs.

DRESSED

"He had been dressed in clothes by the orphanage, but as soon as he was released into the ward he tried to tear them off, chattering and screaming.

"I know monkeys very well, and the sounds he made were the sounds of a frightened monkey attempting to warn his tribe of approaching danger.

"He was very frightened of people, and whenever we came near he would try and climb away. If we tried to catch him, his last line of defence would be to try and bite us.

"When left alone, he would sit in a crouched position and fan his face with his right hand the way that monkeys do. He could not chew and refused to eat meat. He liked soft foods such as mangoes and bananas. Most of all he liked liquid.

"He was very strong, far stronger than a normal child. When he grabbed hold of a bed rail it would take two of us to pull him away. If I picked him up, he would swing so that he faced away from my body and hooked his legs around me. I have seen baby monkeys behave in this way.

HUMAN

"It was obvious that the boy had no knowledge of other human beings. He was terrified of any human who came near him. He was utterly miserable in the ward and it took a long time before he trusted any of the staff.

"His worst moments were when we placed him in a cot. He screamed without stopping, and the only way we could make him stay in the cot was to tie him down.

"After he had been in the ward for some months, he got quite used to this procedure, and when we put him down he would meekly put out his hands to be tied.

"When frightened or excited, he would jump up and down, dash to the other side of the ward and attempt to climb up the window frame.

"He did not seem to hear us when we called him. In spite of our efforts to teach him, he could not say a single word. We thought he might be a deaf-mute.

A WILD BOY IS FOUND

TREATED

"A psychiatrist treated him and it did help a little, but really there was nothing we could do for him. So three months ago he was released into the care of a Roman Catholic orphanage.

"He was a nice little boy, and I sometimes wonder if it would not have been kinder to leave him with the monkeys where he felt he belonged."

The psychiatrist who treated John is Dr. Viatcheslav Zarotchintsev.

"The boy was a very interesting case," he said. "His behaviour was entirely consistent with that of a monkey.

"Books tell us there have been cases of animals saving the lives of little boys and girls, and it is entirely possible that this is what happened here.

"The child is not a deaf-mute as the hospital at first thought. Clinically he is an idiot with an IQ of a one-year-old. It is impossible to say whether he was born abnormal or became abnormal during his life.

"He can hear normally but he is unable to speak.

"I was able to teach him to walk upright, and I taught him toilet training and to be less excitable.

(All this teaching the boy is well and good, but it is obliterating the traces of life in the wild and is destroying his value as a scientific discovery.)

"There is no chance of his recovery and I think it is doubtful he will live beyond his 14th year.

"The saddest thing is that he will never be able to communicate his experiences to us."

Today John lives in an orphanage with 71 other children at the Catholic orphanage in Gitega, 110 km north of Bujumbura.

Petronille Sinibarura is responsible for his care. "When John arrived, he was still an animal in spite of all their efforts in Bujumbura.

"He still had hair covering his body and refused to eat from plates. Whenever we gave him food, he would throw it on the floor and eat it from there.

"We have made a lot of progress in a short time. He now responds to his name and the phrase 'Come and eat.' The hair on his body has disappeared and he will now eat from a plate.

THE WILD BOY OF BURUNDI

LOVE

"The secret is to give him lots of love. He enjoys being held and stroked. He is still far from normal, but he is improving.

"He will never be normal. He still thinks of himself as a monkey. I'm sure that if he had the opportunity he would scamper into the bush. We are very careful never to leave him alone because he is agile enough to climb over the orphanage wall.

"He has abnormal strength for a child of his age and the other children are frightened of him. He has an enormous appetite and eats four times as much as the other children.

"Clinically we have noted that he does not have good eye control. His growth is stunted. He is 90 cm tall and weighs only 20 kg. He is happiest when eating or drinking. He really loves bananas."

I spent several hours observing John. He chatters constantly, making what seem to be monkey sounds. Though he now walks upright, he carries his arms low and stoops so that they sometimes touch the floor. Because of this he still has thick calluses on his hands.

He frightens very easily, and when scared, attempts to run away. When really frightened, he scrambles onto all fours and makes a noise like a monkey scream.

At one point during my visit, John saw a small boy about to eat a banana. Uttering an angry growl, John rushed over to the child and snatched the banana from his hands. It was like watching a monkey in a zoo.

"If anybody doubts this story," said Father Tuhabonye wryly, "they have only to watch John for a few minutes. It is obvious that he models his behaviour on monkeys and considers himself to be a monkey."

When I put the story down, my heart was racing. The tone was sensationalist and the account no doubt popularized, but it was crammed with facts, specific details that could easily be verified and were unlikely to have been fabricated. Even more impressive, John had so many of Victor's traits that they were practically twins. Surely David Barritt, the journalist who'd written the story, hadn't studied the case of the Wild Boy of Aveyron and then attributed to John the hallmarks of Victor's feral upbringing. "He was simply an animal when he arrived," reports the directress of the orphanage in the capital, Bujumbura. How often had that been said of Victor! "John walks on all fours"; so had Victor. So, indeed, had virtually every feral child on record. The record goes back at least to 1735, when Carolus Linnaeus, a Swedish botanist, worked out his monumental scheme for classifying all living things, assigning each to a family, genus, and species—the model biologists still use. Linnaeus thought there should be a separate species for wild men—*Homo ferus*—and pointed out that they were unlike *Homo sapiens* (you and me) in three distinguishing ways. The first of these was *tetrapus:* they walk on all fours. Score one for John. The second was *mutus:* wild men may utter cries, but they have no language. Victor was thought at first to be deaf because, like all wild children we know of, he was mute. And John? "In spite of our efforts to teach him," reports the nurse at the hospital, "he could not say a single word. We thought he might be a deaf-mute." Score two for John. Linnaeus's third and final requirement for belonging to the class of wild men was *hirsutus*—hairy. And here we have John's nurse at the hospital telling us that the boy was originally covered with a fine coat of dark hair on his back and legs, which has since disappeared.

Moreover, like the Wild Boy of Aveyron, John is reportedly afraid of strangers and bites those who come too close. Like Victor, John has marked food preferences. Victor's passion was for acorns and walnuts, both abundant in the forests of central France. John has a passion, it seems, for bananas, ubiquitous in the tropics of Burundi. Neither child would eat meat. I was especially interested to read that John's caretaker at the Gitega orphanage said the boy "does not have good eye control," for Victor, too, had a wandering gaze; scientists who studied him thought he might have acquired the habit of scanning his environment in the forests in order to maintain constant vigilance for predators. Score three more points for John. All things taken together, the story made John out to be as much a feral child as Victor. The story was too good to be true, perhaps, but it certainly rang true in many details.

It was time to do some checking. Peace Corps headquarters in Washington gave me the telephone number of their office in Gaborone, Botswana, and presently I had the director, Charles Taylor's father, on the line. Did he have any first-hand knowledge of the story, I shouted at him transatlantically. No, he did not. Did he know David

Barritt? He had spoken with him on the phone and would give me his number. A few minutes later, I had my first-hand witness on the line in Johannesburg. I explained the scientific interest in his story and asked him which things he had seen himself and which were recounted to him. He had visited the boy for a day in Gitega and decided that the child is completely wild. John fans his face with his hand like a monkey. He utters strange monkey-like chattering noises, but does not speak. He's very excitable when approached. He can't walk properly. He eats only bananas. The Catholic authorities are convinced that he was raised by monkeys.

So far I had merely confirmed Barritt's own words, but next he gave me some valuable insight into conditions in Burundi. He had tried repeatedly to get a visa without success, and when he finally got one, he was turned back upon his arrival at the airport in the capital, Bujumbura. Foreigners, and especially journalists, are not welcome. When at last he did get across the border, he was allowed to stay only three days. In any event, he couldn't interview the soldiers who had captured the boy, since the southwest region is off-limits, probably because of the massacre that took place there during the civil uprisings in 1972. He recommended that I ask for a businessman's visa, get inoculations against yellow fever, typus, typhoid, cholera, smallpox, and polio, start on quinine, bring money, and work through the American embassy. And, oh yes, there's a weekly flight direct to Bujumbura from Brussels.

During the next few hours, I had trouble keeping my mind on affairs in the office. As chairman of the Psychology Department, I had a memo to write defending our budget for the following year. Then there was a meeting of the psychology faculty to discuss the criteria for promotion, a call to entice a coy prospective employee, and an appointment with a dean to ask that a lounge be converted into a classroom. All of these affairs took on more than their usual unreality placed side by side with the struggle of a young boy to survive alone in the wilderness. Centuries of civilization had liberated us from the vicissitudes of nature only to subjugate us to the vicissitudes of bureaucracy—or so it seemed. The fact of the matter was, I had unwittingly begun my

A WILD BOY IS FOUND

journey to Burundi. There was no time to spare. In the first place, now that the story was out, the press would soon trample all over the place and make it difficult or impossible to conduct a careful study. Moreover, I was reliving the fears of the French scientists, over a century and a half ago, who rushed headlong to Aveyron to examine Victor as soon as they had word of his capture; as time passes, the wild boy becomes more acculturated and it becomes more difficult to detect the effects of his life in isolation. Could I make all the necessary preparations in a matter of weeks? Lay down a plan of research, secure funding, obtain visas, assemble supplies? I would certainly try.

II

PREPARATIONS

That evening I learned more about where I was headed from maps and the few sources available in the Boston Public Library. If Africa were a torso, Burundi, in shape and in position, would be its heart. I had imagined a country of dense tropical forests, filled with exotic animals with fearsome names—bassarisks, bandicoots, and betongs—and even more fearsome cries, as predators and prey fought their primeval battles in the sweltering heat. I believe I was indebted for that romantic image to an old film about Stanley and Livingstone. Those intrepid Victorians did in fact pass through northwestern Burundi in the late 1800's. However, I was mistaken about all the rest. Burundi is not sweltering but cool, since it is elevated and mountainous. The jungle forests are gone, cleared by farmers in their efforts to cultivate enough food for a dense and growing population. For much the same reason, there is virtually no wildlife left. I also read that there had been recent civil wars in which over 100,000 people had been massacred.

PREPARATIONS

To supplement this information, Thomas Melady, the former American ambassador to Burundi, told me when I called him in Philadelphia the next day that there were few telephones, little electricity, and only one paved road in this overpopulated, undernourished, and disease-ridden country. It was clear that if I was going to conduct a definitive scientific study of a wild boy in Burundi, I would need a lot of advice—technical, medical, and political—and a lot of collaboration. Most important, the project should be jointly undertaken by a psychologist and a physician. Surely the consequences of prolonged isolation were physiological as well as behavioral. Moreover, the debate that has raged over Victor in the past two centuries has been as much medical as psychological. Was he simply retarded since birth, or did he become that way through isolation? Perhaps he was left to survive in the wild when his parents discovered he was retarded, so he was both brain-damaged and feral. Or did he suffer from the childhood disease known as autism, which just as surely isolates the child psychologically from those around him, although he remains in their midst? The same questions would be asked of John; we had to have the medical facts to answer them. Moreover, I might need a doctor myself before the project was finished. I would surely need a friend, so I asked Dr. Richard Pillard to join me in studying John of Burundi.

Richard is a tall, slightly balding man in his early forties. His brisk gait, sturdy build, unpretentious clothes, and serene face exude confidence. I have often seen him laugh but never cry, often seen him delighted but seldom angry. When you speak to him, he listens as much with his eyes, fixed squarely on you, as with his ears. When he speaks to you, it is simple, direct, frank. In short, he is the very model of a modern psychiatrist. Unlike many therapists, though, he is a scientist, impatient with mentalistic mumbo-jumbo. He likes to use his deductive powers to unravel any interesting tangle, whether it concerns language, human relationships, or the effects of psychoactive drugs (his specialty as part of the medical faculty at Boston University). So I knew that the idea of studying the Wild Boy of Burundi would intrigue him. "The idea itself struck me as wild," he later wrote in his diary. "Was there really such a boy? Could we get the funds to examine him?

Would the Burundi government let us in? Would those who care for the boy cooperate?"

Benn Shedd asked me many of the same questions when I called him at WGBH, Boston's educational TV station. A month earlier, we had discussed making a television documentary on the Wild Boy of Aveyron for the highly acclaimed *Nova* series, of which Benn is a producer. Now I had a proposal for him. We would want the most sophisticated photodocumentation possible on John of Burundi: close-ups of his head, eyes, skin, teeth, and gums. Films of his gait, his skilled movements, his responses to our tests, his fanning, and his mouth movements during chattering, accompanied of course by an audio track. And much more. Neither Richard nor I is expert in film-making, hence my proposal: *Nova* would work with us on the project, provide the documentation required, and in the process obtain enough footage to make an eyewitness report of a scientific investigation. It would mean film-making under impossibly difficult conditions, but it would also allow the public to see, whether John proves a jungle boy or a myth, what research is like in progress—its flounderings, its false scents, and its victories. Benn was interested. To begin with, he wanted to know what kinds of tests we planned to run on the boy and what we wanted documented. Fair enough. We didn't know where the money was coming from, or if we could get visas, or if the local authorities would permit the research, but suppose all that worked out—what, indeed, would we do with the jungle boy once we reached him?

Benn proposed that we discuss plans over dinner, and some hours later Richard and I met him in the lobby of a downtown hotel. When we were settled at the table, I suggested that, to start with, we review the tests that had been conducted the last time a wild boy had been studied systematically—in 1800! The subject of the study was, of course, the Wild Boy of Aveyron. When the boy was captured in the south of France, one Citizen Bonnaterre, a high school biology teacher there, undertook an exhaustive study of the boy that lasted several months. For Bonnaterre, as for every scholar of that time, including the Wild Boy's future teacher, Jean-Marc Itard, the senses were the portals of the mind; all knowledge was acquired through the senses. It was

natural, then, that Bonnaterre began by observing the boy in the
minutest detail, and also natural that the emphasis of his study was on
the boy's senses. This view, which placed life's experiences (the things
we see, hear, touch, and so on) above all else in shaping man, above
his intuitions, his native abilities, his biological constitution—this view
was the heritage of the great Enlightenment philosopher Etienne Bon-
not de Condillac, who wrote: "Nothing is known to us except through
our senses." Of course, the experiential view of human nature did not
begin with Condillac; he took it largely from his English counterpart,
John Locke. But when French scholars formed the first anthropological
society, wrote the first book on psychiatry, conducted experiments in
clinical medicine, educated the deaf, or trained the Wild Boy of Aveyron in the early nineteenth century, Condillac was their guide. Conse-
quently, he has become our guide as well: only three lifetimes separate
him from us. Sensory training seemed a radically fresh approach to
Bonnaterre and Itard; nowadays, we can scarcely think of any other way
to go about the education of the retarded, the deaf, or indeed, the
normal preschool child. The chapters of Bonnaterre's report on the
Wild Boy of Aveyron were titled: external appearance, gait, sensory
process, speech deprivation, instinct, nourishment, suspicion of imbecility, character, regimen, comparison with other wild children.

We decided that Bonnaterre's program for studying Victor and
ours for studying John need not be that different. For one thing,
Bonnaterre was largely right: many of the most interesting changes that
life in the wild brought about in Victor had to do with his senses. He
was indifferent to temperature and rejected clothing even in the coldest
weather; he would put his hand in a fire; his eyes didn't fixate; he
reached alike for painted objects, objects in relief, and the image of
objects reflected in a mirror; he didn't sneeze even with snuff, nor did
he weep; he didn't respond to loud noises; he didn't recognize edible
food by sight, but by smell; he preferred uncooked food and had no
taste for sweets or hard drink; he had no emotional ties, no sexual
expression, no speech; he had a peculiar gait and would occasionally run
on all fours.

We would want to study John's vision (like Victor, he reportedly has a wandering gaze); observe how he coordinates sight and hand movements (Victor had excellent skilled movements, and this is one bit of evidence that he wasn't severely retarded); check his pupillary reflex as a sign of neurological disorder. We must test his hearing (like Victor, he was initially thought deaf, since he doesn't speak) and record his voice, especially the monkeylike sounds so that we can compare them later with the chattering of the grey enkende monkeys. We need to know more about how he chooses foods (Victor selected foods by smell more than by sight, always sniffing his food before eating it), and will want to examine his teeth and gums (Victor's gums were lacerated). We wondered what sort of relationship John had with those who cared for him. Did he, like Victor, love his teacher and exert himself to learn? How would he react to the other children in the orphanage and to us as strangers? What emotions would he display? A problem which concerned us was whether we would be misled by what we saw. The behavior of a normal Burundi child would almost certainly be different from that of an American child. Would we be able to appreciate this? We are not anthropologists, yet we need to understand the behavior of a unique child in a foreign culture.

There were, of course, tests we hoped to conduct that Bonnaterre could not—for example, X-rays, blood and urine tests (how do you collect a urine sample from a wild child?), films of movement in the dark. And we expected to rely on yet another gift of modern science in order to peer in every cavity of an uncooperative hyperactive child —tranquilizers. Finally, I made a note to read up on Bantu phonology and the behavior of enkende monkeys. I thought I had better learn something about the sounds in Bantu languages, since if John had been a normal child abandoned at the age of four, as Barritt's article suggests, he must have spoken Rundi (which belongs to the Bantu family), and perhaps some of the vowels and consonants of his native language survive in his inarticulate chattering. And we had better learn something about his foster parents, the grey enkendes, since if John was their adopted child he probably learned many of their mannerisms—grooming, fighting off aggressors, scavenging for food and so on. These were our first thoughts on what to do when we met John—assuming we met him. Benn was intrigued but cautious.

PREPARATIONS

"It's a bigger project than *Nova* usually undertakes," he said. "We would need a five-man crew, and it could cost us a quarter of a million dollars." He said he would check it out with his executive producer, but he wasn't optimistic. "Would you risk that kind of money on the strength of a newspaper article?"

Over cheesecake and espresso we agreed that the next step was to get the advice of experts in several specialties. Boston is teeming with experts on every conceivable subject and jungle boys have a certain fascination for everyone, so it was not difficult to assemble the right group in my home the following Sunday evening. Richard was the first to arrive, carrying a cassette recorder. He intended to document the complete oral history of our research, he explained—not only the studies in Burundi but the planning stages as well.

SUNDAY, MAY 9 — BOSTON
From Richard's diary

I guess I was early for the meeting at Harlan's because I was so excited at the prospect of the trip. Still, there were reasons to restrain my enthusiasm. In the end, we might not be able to go, since we had neither funds nor visas, and neither would be easy to get. Then, too, I felt that my training as a psychiatrist was not the ideal one for this mission; a pediatrician might be a better choice. Lastly, John might prove, of course, not to be a feral child at all—but that was all right; this was a problem that needed a solution, and working out that solution would be reward enough.

Before the guests came, Harlan and I talked about other matters. He is forty, something of an ectomorph, a little shorter than my six feet. He has black bushy hair, rather French features, but in fact he's from Russian stock. Professionally, Harlan is a cross between a psychologist and a linguist. At Harvard in the 1960's, he was a student of B. F. Skinner, which makes him more sanguine than I am about solving the problems of mankind by changing human behavior. Nowadays he is working on the American Sign Language of the Deaf—which you can tell at a glance, since his hands rarely stop moving in a conversation and his face is much more expressive than is usually allowed in our

Anglo-Saxon corner of the world. His speech is peppered with French phrases, a vestige of the four or five years he spent living in France and teaching the psychology of language at the Sorbonne. From the time we met three years ago I liked his quick intelligence, his ability to manage in any situation, his unfailing sense of humor. Our professional interests as psychologist and psychiatrist are complementary and often lead us, to the irritation of our companions, into long and absorbing conversations. Beyond that is the unnameable chemistry which almost at once turned us into trusting friends.

When all the others had arrived, there were nine of us: Martin Moore-Ede, a physiologist from Harvard; Peter Rosenberger, a pediatric neurologist; Alex Skavenski, a psychologist and an expert on eye movement; Larry Stoddard, an authority on behavior of the retarded; Mike Terman, whose specialty is biological rhythms; Jackie and Benn Shedd, Harlan, and me. Except for Benn, whose attitude was hard to read, the group was less skeptical about our expedition than I had expected. They knew the odds that John wouldn't be a feral child, but no one doubted that the story deserved to be investigated as rigorously as possible. We had a fine brainstorming session and came away three hours later with a list of things to do that didn't leave much out.

• Conduct a complete physical and neurological examination of the boy. We must assemble the necessary examining instruments, including spare bulbs and batteries, since it is likely that we will have nothing to work with in Burundi.

• Take complete measurements, including weight, head and chest circumference, crown-rump span, arm span, standing and sitting height. These measurements will give us an idea of how much John is retarded in physical growth. In addition, abnormal bone growth, especially enlargement of the head, accompanies many forms of mental retardation and could indicate that John has brain damage.

• Examine his teeth, photograph them, and make a bite cast if possible. Careful study of John's teeth could provide information about his diet and manner of feeding. This would be a piece of evidence in determining how long he has lived in the forest.

• Take X-rays of long bones, chest, skull, and teeth. These will be

PREPARATIONS

important because a child's age can be determined quite precisely from the degree of fusion of the epiphyses, the growth buds at the ends of the long bones. Also, deformities of the skull might point to certain kinds of mental retardation or to a head injury. There should be an X-ray machine somewhere near the orphanage, but then again we aren't even certain that the area has electricity.

• Collect blood and urine specimens for any evidence they might give about John's nutrition and general health. Hormone levels might show the effects of prolonged stress. Some types of mental retardation are associated with abnormal products of metabolism that also show up in the urine.

• Make detailed observations of his behavior. There are systems for observing child behavior and recording it in minute detail on something like a stenotype machine, but we will be content with written notes and running dictation on a pocket tape recorder. Of course we will also have films of his gait and movements that we can analyze later. We agreed that it would be good to have observations and possibly films of his sleeping and his activity in the dark.

• Make sound recordings of his vocalizations on good portable equipment. Can we get a recording of monkey chatter to play for John?

• Conduct a sensory examination. This will be both important and difficult; it is hard enough to do on a normal, cooperative child. There are a variety of sophisticated ways to measure hearing in a child who won't follow instructions, but they generally require equipment we can't take with us and a degree of compliance we aren't likely to get from John. Simple instruments like a tuning fork and a rattle will be enough. Sense of smell? We will take various odorous chemicals to give us a rough idea of John's olfactory acuity. Testing the adequacy of vision requires a roomful of equipment and a specialist in nothing but that: sharpness of focus, color and depth perception, the pupils' reaction to light, the extent of the visual fields, the integrity of the nerves and muscles controlling conjugate eye movements—we will do our best to examine them all.

The assembled scientists offered many more suggestions. Examine his food preferences; see if he will learn in return for rewards of food;

get an enkende monkey and put him with John. Someone wondered
how we would interpret the height and size measurements, since these
would naturally depend on John's tribal origins. How reliably could you
distinguish a Mututsi from a Muhutu from a pygmy Mutwa?* Maybe
the blood typing would help with that. Another good suggestion was
to examine a second child at the orphanage who was the same age as
John so that we would have a standard of physique and behavior by
which to make comparisons. Researchers often make use of a "match-
ing" procedure like this; it would help us to see what behavior is normal
for a Murundi eight years old.

During the evening, Harlan distributed some proof sheets of
photos he had just received from Barritt at the *Johannesburg Times.*
A few of the pictures we recognized from his article. Benn Shedd
looked at the sheets intently. "Not much here," he said, "this looks like
a fairly normal kid." This was our fear too: we would arrive and find
a normal child with a vague history of having lived with monkeys.

Benn's initial enthusiasm seems to have subsided; citing the small
budgets of educational programs, he now offers us only a camera and
instructions on its use. Sounds like his boss is down on the project, and
I am dismayed. Film documentation will probably be one of the most
important kinds of data we collect, and we want it to be of better
quality than home movies.

The evening ended with a useful offer from Peter Rosenberger.
So that we can get practice examining an uncooperative child, Peter
will ask the Fernald School for retarded children with which he is
affiliated to allow us to give a routine physical to a child with a difficult
behavior problem.

MONDAY, MAY 10—BOSTON

This afternoon, Richard came by so we could drive to the Fernald
School together. Before leaving, I called Benn Shedd and found his
feathers very ruffled. Benn had felt distinctly left out at last evening's

*In the Kirundi language, the prefix *mu* denotes the singular, *ba*, the plural. A member
of the Tutsi tribe is a Mututsi; more than one are Batutsi. The uninflected form is used
here as an adjective: Tutsi leaders.

meeting. Clearly photodocumentation will be important and I said so, but I also said that *Nova* was "chickening out of the expedition," a comment I now regret. Benn had been planning on at least giving us some good photo gear and training us in its use. Now I don't know.

At the school, we found Peter Rosenberger, who promptly led us to the child he had chosen for our practice examination. Her name is Paula, and she is a profoundly retarded girl about fourteen years old with the intelligence of a two-year-old. Paula is easily agitated; she slapped and bit herself while we tried to examine her. However, with patience and Peter's expert help, we did manage a reasonable neurological examination. Glancing at the other children on the ward, we realized that many of them behaved in ways that would be hard to distinguish from what we had heard about John. Even Paula showed no particular neurological deficits beyond an awkward gait and poor coordination.

Paula suffers from an illness called phenylketonuria, which is a common cause of mental retardation and might even be the reason for John's symptoms. Children like Paula lack an enzyme needed to form protein from phenylalanine, a protein building block in the diet. Without the critical enzyme, phenylalanine is changed into phenylketones, which are poisonous to the brain and cause the tragic retardation we are seeing—all the more tragic in Paula's case because, about the time she was born, researchers learned how to diagnose this condition at birth and to prevent its damaging effects by feeding the child a diet free of phenylalanine.

Peter continued his helpfulness by giving us some supplies for drawing blood and by writing to the American ambassador in Burundi to say that if John returns with us to the United States, the Shriver Center at the Fernald School would accept him as a patient. The Northeastern Press Bureau had sent a photographer to cover our dry run, but as we did not wish to have Paula photographed for publicity, we sent him away. We left not long after, as I had to make a meeting of my college's tenure and promotion committee; my heart wasn't in it.

During the meeting my thoughts turned to the next obstacle separating us from John: we had no funds for supplies and travel. Now that Richard and I had refined our plans and pretested our examination, we could describe exactly what we planned to do, but who would provide us with the funds to do it, and how quickly? The obvious sponsors for this research were the National Institutes of Health—either the Institute of Child Health and Human Development, which last year spent some 12 million dollars on behavioral research, or the Institute of Mental Health, which spent 65 million dollars on grants to investigators. We estimated that we would need a paltry five thousand dollars, mainly to pay the air fare from Boston to Bujumbura (and back!), and to buy medical and other supplies. But the Institutes of Health were out of the question because of their ponderously slow review process. The next deadline for applications was a full two months off, the period for review eight months, and even then many an investigator during the Nixon and Ford administrations received a letter saying that his or her grant was approved but the funding delayed for an unknown period. While Washington shuffled papers, John would become increasingly socialized, and by the time we received the funds it might well be impossible to tell if he had ever been a feral child —if indeed we could find him. Victor managed to evade surveillance and escape back into the forest three times. Freedom might be John's first priority, too.

There is, however, a small grants program in the National Institute of Mental Health to aid the young investigator in launching his research career or following up an initial discovery. Since the amounts of the awards are small, the reasoning goes, the review of the proposal can be more rapid. The time from application to award is only a year! But surely, you say, a government that can launch a nuclear war in an hour can in a day or so find a few thousand dollars to explore a possible scientific discovery. There are highly placed administrators with limited discretionary funds for research that must be initiated immediately, right? Wrong.

The director of the William T. Grant Foundation, Philip Sapir, knew this when I called him and related the story of John the Jungle Boy and our proposed investigation. If John is a feral child, his discovery can be one of the most important in the behavioral sciences in this century. The opportunity may not arise again for another century and a half, if ever. If John is not feral, we need to know that, too; the case must be closed. The Grant Foundation is a private philanthropy that since it began in 1936 has supported research on child development. It is supporting the study of Genie, a girl raised in isolation in an attic room by emotionally disturbed parents. It is obviously the appropriate sponsor for our project. We need five thousand dollars within a week. To my immense relief, Philip Sapir agreed. I was to send him immediately a written description of the project and a detailed budget.

I made plane reservations for Bujumbura for the following week, allowing a stopover in Paris to obtain visas. Since learning from David Barritt how the Burundi government felt about visitors, I had also heard another chilling tale. A friend had met a cameraman in a bar in Philadelphia who said that a few months earlier he and a reporter had been stopped by soldiers on a country road in Burundi and his companion had been ordered out of the jeep and summarily shot. The narrator escaped by dashing across a field, dropping his cameras and film case as he ran. While I didn't give the story much credence, I was also not optimistic about our promptly getting visas in Washington as American investigators. My plan was to try and get them in Paris—more neutral ground—and if we failed, to ask friends at UNESCO to intercede on our behalf, perhaps even sponsor the mission officially. I had my laissez-passer from the days I had traveled for UNESCO in West Africa, and I hoped vaguely that it would somehow persuade people to let us pass.

Besides, I have had a decade-old love affair with Paris and somewhat briefer affairs with a few of its inhabitants. It is the most cultured city in the world, the apogee of what society has to offer in literature, art, architecture, food, dress. The city of Hugo, Toulouse-Lautrec, Escoffier, Cardin—what better point of departure for studying a wild child utterly cut off from society. Then, too, I knew a Parisian anthropologist who had spent some time in Rwanda, Burundi's neighbor.

WEDNESDAY, MAY 12—WASHINGTON

Richard stopped by last night while I was distracting my feverish brain with *Cool Hand Luke* (a movie on TV); earlier in the day I'd had my yellow fever shot. As we were drawing up our packing list, Benn Shedd called to say that *Nova* had pulled out completely. The ostensible reason is that the stills taken by David Barritt show too socialized a child. Perhaps there is no wild child, they fear, or one who has lost all his wild behavior and would yield poor footage. They miss the point, of course: properly done, the story can't fail because it is about the conduct of inquiry. No doubt they would have refused to accompany Stanley because he might not have found Livingstone. In any case, Benn has advised us on cameras and films: an Elmo Super 8 motion picture camera with sound, high-speed Ektachrome film and a Polaroid camera for stills. If I get the equipment and do a test run, Benn will arrange to look at some of our footage before we leave.

For some time, Richard and I had been debating the best strategy to get our visas. My plan was to avoid any dealings with our own State Department or the Burundi consulate here, proceeding directly to Paris to obtain our visas there. Richard was afraid, however, that we would run into snags and be stuck in Paris squandering the foundation's money; I was less punctilious, knowing how pleasant it is to be stuck in Paris. As it turned out, events overtook us and changed our plans. Two days ago I had cabled David Kaeuper at the American embassy in Bujumbura—David Barritt had given me his name—asking that John's caretaker, Father Tuhabonye, wire us a request for medical assistance. This was to aid in getting the visas. Kaeuper's reply came back via the State Department. David Cardwell, the Burundi desk officer, called me to relay it:

> TUHABONYE FOR THE MOMENT IS IN THE INTERIOR
> BEYOND THE REACH OF THE GITEGA MISSION.
> EMBASSY HAS ASKED MISSION TO HAVE HIM CONTACT
> KAEUPER SOONEST REGARDING CONTENTS OF LANE
> TELEGRAM.

Cardwell was very understanding of our mission and urged us to apply for visas in Washington; he agreed to pave the way with a call to the Burundi chargé d'affaires, Dr. Clement Sambira. I then had a lengthy and pleasant chat with him on the phone, full of *"nous serions extrêmement reconnaissant's."* The outcome: Richard and I met early this morning, and prepared with three passport photos, a rendezvous at ten-thirty at the Burundi embassy, and the hope of getting our visas, we set out for Washington. I still felt wretched from the yellow fever shot, but Richard was positively loquacious. First he proposed that when we saw Sambira, we broach the question of bringing the boy back. Then, too, that we quiz David Cardwell at State on that issue and on X-ray facilities, freezers, ice, electric current, clothing, acceptability of beards, and religious orders of orphanages in Bujumbura and Gitega.

As we began our descent into Washington, I tried to imagine the sights and the feelings I would experience descending into Bujumbura only a week later—if all went well at the Burundi consulate.

It did. The consulate is in a modest row building. The interior is very simply furnished, even a bit shabby. These diplomats' standard of living seemed about that of an American office worker. Evidently, Burundi had no money to squander on empty appearances. We waited only a moment in the consulate lobby. Dr. Sambira and a visa official received us. I briefly explained in French what we were hoping to do. We completed forms and were given visas in a matter of minutes, without even paying the usual seven-dollar fee—easier than getting a parking sticker at Northeastern University.

While waiting for the documents to be stamped, we glanced at a tourist book on Burundi. The landscape is beautiful, but it was hard to decide about the city of Bujumbura. Our prospective hotel, the Paguidas, didn't look like much. Nothing looked like much.

We took a taxi to David Cardwell's office at the State Department. He is a young, very handsome and polished black man whose sensitivity impressed us both. He had recently returned from Burundi and had even been to Gitega but not to the orphanage which was our destination. He began by saying that he was pleased at how the Burundi officials had treated us. The State Department had been attempting to improve relations after Secretary Kissinger's visit, and the prompt assistance given us was taken as the first sign that the Burundi government was responding. Cardwell showed us his cables to David Kaeuper, the economic attaché in Bujumbura, who would meet our plane and help with arrangements. He mentioned that the rainy season was late this year—it was just starting when he left Burundi at the end of April, so we will catch the end of it during our stay. Finally, Cardwell also said that he had caught malaria and had been very sick. He was just now about to stop taking chloroquine and would know in a few weeks if he would have a relapse.

Cardwell's story was sobering, but nevertheless we were exhilarated as we left the State Department. Everything was turning out perfectly. Coming back from Logan Airport we decided to stop at Air France for tickets. While we examined schedules, a screech of tires startled us. Outside a woman had been struck by a car. Richard rushed up to her as she lay on the street, in shock but not, he judged by a quick examination, seriously injured. It was the day's second reminder of our vulnerability.

THURSDAY, MAY 13 — BOSTON
From Richard's diary

We are leaving a week from today, and we must get together the medicines and supplies we will need. I called a doctor at the World Health Organization who had been to Burundi, but he wasn't reassuring. His advice: Don't go to Burundi. If you go, don't get sick; if you get sick, treat yourself; if you can't treat yourself, get out. More advice: bring gifts to ingratiate yourselves (balls, T-shirts, money), and of course, don't drink the water.

We have begun our immunizations. Yellow fever, smallpox, typhoid, typhus and tetanus. The typhoid vaccine left us weak and feverish for twenty-four hours and our arms are still sore, but it's better than getting typhoid.

Malaria is common in Burundi; in fact it is one of the commonest and most ravaging diseases known. Malaria victims suffer terrible sweats and fever every three or four days and sometimes contract jaundice. Having just experienced our own bout with fever

PREPARATIONS

after the shots, we could appreciate how debilitating it would be. There is no immunization against malaria, no way to prevent it except to spray and eradicate the anopheles mosquito carrier. When these mosquitoes bite, they inject parasites into the bloodstream that live in the red blood cells. Some of the infected cells are taken back by other mosquitoes when they bite the same person, so the malaria parasite can continue its life cycle. This endless chain—man-mosquito-man-mosquito—is known to have devastated early civilizations in tropical regions.

Malaria is not usually fatal (if it were, the parasite would die with its victims). In time, the natural defenses of the body will bring about a cure, but in epidemic areas people are constantly reinfected and thus are often sick. There is, however, chloroquine (related to quinine), a medication that suppresses the symptoms until the body can get rid of the parasite. We must take chloroquine tablets once a week before, during and after we have been in the infected area. Sometimes that isn't enough and one gets sick anyway, as happened to David Cardwell.

What other medications should we take? We tried to think of all the bad things that could happen, and if there was a treatment, we took it. Little items are most often overlooked:

Chapped lips: Chapstick
Sunburn: Solarcaine
Sore feet: Foot powder
Insect noises: 6–12 insect repellent
Insect bites: Hydrocortisone cream and antiseptic cream
Upset stomach: Alka-Seltzer
Border woes: Aspirin

For more serious problems:

Lomotil for the African counterpart of Montezuma's revenge
Penicillin and tetracycline for infections
Compazine for nausea
Secobarbital in case we had to sleep in uncomfortable quarters
Dextroamphetamine to fight exhaustion
Kwel lotion for lice

Demerol, a good painkiller for something serious like a broken
bone

So much for us. For John we decided on:

Benadryl and Valium to calm him down (possibly also to calm us
down)

Cyclogel to dilate his pupils so that we can examine his eyes

Mellaril, an antipsychotic drug, in case John's symptoms resemble
those of schizophrenia

Next came the equipment we would need to examine John.
With *Nova*'s brusque withdrawal, we would need a motion picture
camera of our own, and a tripod, a still camera, a dental camera for
extreme close-ups, and a Polaroid for immediate results—check.
And two hundred rolls of motion picture film, indoor and outdoor
still film, Polaroid film, a flash and flashcubes and penlite batteries,
and a portable tape recorder that runs on batteries, and the batteries, and audio tape, and an empty reel—check. But what else? An
ophthalmoscope-otoscope, for peering in John's eyes and ears. A
tuning fork to test hearing and sensitivity to vibration. A stetho-
scope, a thermometer and a sphygmomanometer to measure blood
pressure. A neurological hammer to test his reflexes. Injection syringes, a tourniquet and alcohol sponges to draw blood; five kinds
of vacuum tubes to store it in; slides and covers to smear it on.
Ten urine sample bottles. Preservative for urine. A serrated tracing
wheel and a pin to test his skin sensitivity. A little red ball to
check his peripheral vision, a piece of striped cloth to check his
eye-movement reflexes, and a flashlight to check his pupillary reflex
(and find our way in the bush). Throat sticks, measuring tape, adhesive tape and Band-Aids. Dental retractors and a dental mirror.
Glucose sticks to test his urine for diabetes, and PKU sticks to test
it for signs of phenylketonuria. Amyl acetate to test his sense of
smell, and M & M's because they taste good and never melt in
your hands while you're doling them out. And string and adhesive
and cotton balls and gauze and Q-tips and a stopwatch, and a knife
on general principles. And a soccer ball to make friends at the orphanage, and a Frisbee in case we can't inflate the soccer ball (will
history remember us as the men who brought Frisbee to Africa?).

PREPARATIONS

Congratulations, you have ten cases of equipment and are three hundred pounds overweight, but you're ready to go. Just one detail: don't forget your personal effects—clothing, documents, toiletries. We took as little as possible. Harlan took his I'm-respectable-so-please-give-me-permission suit, I packed my Dictaphone.

Everyone is interested in our trip and is truly generous with time and information. Ray Williams, a charming Southerner who is a research dentist at Harvard, spent an evening showing me how to take a competent set of full-mouth photographs. It's a two-man job: one inserts a set of polished steel mirrors in the patient's mouth and the other shoots with a camera built for super close-ups. Next morning at the lab I tried the system on my technician, Mike, and by noon had the film in the tubs of a four-hour developing service. That night we reviewed Mike's teeth in fine detail and living color. Not a perfect job but good enough to assure that I could handle the equipment.

What about getting blood samples out of Burundi? Blood has to be frozen, and I'm sure there won't be a freezer at the orphanage— perhaps not even at the hospital in Bujumbura. And a centrifuge! You have to separate plasma from red cells within a few hours after you draw the blood; otherwise the red cells burst and interfere with the analysis. There must be a centrifuge in Bujumbura if they do any blood chemistries . . . but what if they don't do any? The last time I had to cope with blood was fifteen years ago as an intern at Boston City Hospital —come to think of it, a jungle of sorts in itself. Boston City is next door to my lab, and Bill Adams, whom I knew from intern days, is the chief of hematology there. A color photo of the Himalayas, peaks rising snow-covered through the clouds, was hanging in Bill's office. It turned out that he had been on a research expedition to Nepal and had faced the same problem we have. To freeze a blood sample, he explained, pack it in a styrofoam box with dry ice—carbon dioxide frozen solid at 109°F below zero. There had not been a dry ice machine anywhere around Nepal or India and there probably won't be where we are going, but all the transcontinental jets carry it. They freeze the packaged meals, then heat them in microwave ovens on the aircraft. Tell the steward you have a medical sample; he will get you a styrofoam box and dry ice to put in it. That was helpful information; now I know why in-flight food tastes the way it does. Bill also supplied technical advice on what preservatives to use for the samples and wondered if we couldn't find a place on this trip for a hematologist.

Thursday is the evening I take my daughters to dinner, and I wanted to see them despite all we have yet to do to prepare for the trip. Ten-year-old Eliza agreed to be our subject for a practice physical exam, so after dinner I looked at her tonsils and tapped her knees while Harlan took movies. Our Super 8 camera records sound while it films and has a zoom lens which gets you as close as twelve inches. After five reels under various conditions of lighting, Harlan was shooting like a pro.

After I had taken the kids back to their mother's in Cambridge, Harlan and I talked about the media interest our trip is generating. So many reporters are calling that neither of us dares answer the phone. Why didn't we anticipate that everyone else would be as interested in this project as we are? Northeastern had slated the press conference for Monday but now wants it moved up to tomorrow at two—okay with us. Harlan is disturbed by rumors that journalists are trying to get into Burundi. I can imagine what it will be like examining John with twenty photographers looking over both shoulders and between my legs. We will let David Cardwell know that we would consider reporters a serious hindrance to the mission.

FRIDAY, MAY 14—BOSTON

The pace this morning at Northeastern was as hectic as I had feared, thanks to calls nonstop from press, radio stations and wire services, all of which I referred to Tom Sprague at the press bureau. A press conference is set for 2:00 P.M., but reporters are trying to get advance word. Tom is upset because a secretary told reporters that I was in but unavailable, whereas he had lied and said I was out of town. One reporter got through by claiming she was a student who needed advice on courses.

A vice-president called to say he had read and signed my grant proposal. I called the foundation to ask if I might mention their name at the conference. Philip Sapir is out of town and his associate is ill, so a secretary and I decided I wouldn't. Same sort of call to Peter Rosenberger at the Eunice Kennedy Shriver Center, which has agreed to care for the boy if we bring him back—same decision.

The press conference was dazzling only because of the TV lights; the questions were predictable. I tossed the medical ones to Richard, who perspired more than he spoke. For backdrop, there were some large maps that predated Burundi's independence and blowups of Barritt's feature story.

Sprague and team snapped the leash back on and led me to an office where we returned calls to radio shows live and network officers dead. Kept a list: KAKE, Witchita (I don't even know how to spell the place); WMEX, Boston; WBEW, Buffalo; WESO, New Orleans—these were live. On tape: UPI, New York; AP, Boston; CBS Radio; Canadian Broadcasting. I'm to be on WBUR on Monday and Avi Nelson, a local talk show, on Wednesday. Oh, I forgot to say I was live on BMIQ in—are you ready?—Winnipeg. NBC called to ask that I take along their 16mm camera, shoot some reels for them and send the film out a day after arriving. They magnanimously offered to pay for the air freight. I refused. CBS called minutes later with the same request plus a cassette recorder and asked that I not mention this to NBC or ABC. My counterproposal was that they lend us a 16mm camera and a Nagra tape recorder and that they give us the necessary film and tape, pay for all our overweight and pool the results with the other networks. "We really hate to pool"—long pause, silence from me —"but I think we can work this one out."

On the way home, I saw Peter Rosenberger at the Massachusetts General Hospital, who gave us some urine bottles, throat sticks and a few other small supplies. Back at the house, our tenant, a psychology student named Vince Ollivier, has tracked down a Catholic order that may run the mission and orphanage in Gitega. They are the White Fathers, and their superior is a Reverend Paul G. Sorelle. I'll call him tomorrow; perhaps he will give me a letter of introduction to the bishop of Bujumbura (or Gitega?). Checked with Alex Skavenski, who is trying to find an enkende monkey, or failing that, a primatologist who knows about them.

THE WILD BOY OF BURUNDI

Marc Onigman, psychology's administrative officer, kindly ran downtown and had the film developed from last night's trial run on Richard's daughter Eliza. Richard and I reviewed the film after supper and were quite satisfied, but I'll call Benn Shedd and ask him to critique it for us.

We spent the rest of the evening going over our equipment inventory, imagining every step of our procedure and what we might need, assuming that nothing would be available at the orphanage. The blood examination alone, for example, requires a tourniquet, foil-wrapped alcohol swabs, needles, syringes, tubes with anticoagulants and five types of preservatives, blood slides and cover slips, pipettes and detailed instructions on separating, preserving and analyzing the blood. We finished about midnight with a toast of our antimalaria drug—you take it once a week and today's the day. Richard says it doesn't prevent malaria, just suppresses the symptoms, but the malaria eventually goes away if you eventually go away from the mosquitoes. The gin is quite optional.

SATURDAY, MAY 15—BOSTON

Alex Skavenski put me onto Peter Marler at Rockefeller University, who has generously been following up the monkey angle. Barritt's article says the boy was caught running with a troop of grey enkende monkeys. Also that he chatters like a monkey and exhibits other monkeylike behavior. Could John turn out to be the first proven case of a child raised by another species? We will want to make good recordings of the child and a monkey—hence the need for the Nagra. Also plan to confront the child with a monkey, in the fanciful hope that they'll hold a conversation or groom each other or God knows what. Marler is now convinced that the enkende (a local label) is related to the vervet, a species of the genus *Cercopithecus*. The world's authority on these seeming homophiles, says Marler, is Tom Struhsaker, off in the bush somewhere in Uganda. Marler has cabled him asking him to call me so I can persuade him to join us in Burundi. Yet I fear it might be a hellish trip for him and possibly for nothing. The responsibility of

PREPARATIONS

taking him away from his work weighs heavily on me; perhaps we can make a final decision after I see the boy. Struhsaker's apparently published sound spectrographs of the vervet's vocalizing, so we can match them up with John's and those I hope to make of the monkeys myself. Marler mentions Richard Leakey in Nairobi for general savvy on zoology in these parts.

Spent most of the day on errands for the trip. Bought a soccer ball and Frisbee for the kids at the orphanage (David Cardwell's suggestion) and ponchos, a hunting knife (Lord knows why), zebra-striped cloth (one yard—useful for testing eye movements), lots of mosquito repellent, but no metal shaving mirror to be had. It feels like I'm preparing for Boy Scout camp. I still need to get my smallpox this week, but Richard shot mc full of typhus.

MONDAY, MAY 17—BOSTON

An exhilarating, exhausting day that began with insomnia, hence an early start at the office. Yesterday I spent the entire day catching up on administrative work and going over a manuscript, with my colleague François Grosjean, on syntax in American Sign Language; Ivy DeRosier, our administrative secretary, is hidden by the stack of paperwork I left. Fred Skinner called, and I filled him in on all that had followed from his call of just two weeks ago. He was very pleased and attached great importance to our mission. Tom Struhsaker called from Fort Portal, Uganda, in response to Peter Marler's cable. I described John's monkey symptoms according to Barritt and the tests and recordings Richard and I plan. Tom clearly shares our sense of excitement and agrees to come to Burundi on demand. I am to cable him when we are ready for his assistance—in identifying the species of monkey John ran with, in evaluating John's monkeyshines, in recording his vocalizations and those of the enkendes, and finally in arranging a tête-à-tête between them and John.

Peter Simmons, the foreign editor for ABC-TV, called to announce they were sending a film crew in to join us. I was violently opposed, explained that he jeopardized our scientific and medical mission as well as the safety of his own personnel. He was unimpressed—said newsmen frequently took personal risks. I called Richard, who was also distressed and agreed with me that the presence of photographers could get us all booted out of the country or worse. We decided to call Cardwell at State and ask him to dissociate us from any journalists vis-à-vis the Burundi authorities. I had to insist on getting his home number from his secretary; he agreed to cable Kaeuper with that information. Then Tom Sprague called to say that ABC had been refused visas after all (but they may be lying). No word yet from Simmons's counterpart at CBS, Fetters, who is arranging a 16mm camera and a Nagra recorder for us. I called the Reverend Sorelle of the White Fathers of Africa, explained our mission and asked if the orphanage at Gitega was under their auspices. He did not know and agreed to check.

At 10:00 A.M. I was interviewed on *This AM,* a Canadian coast-to-coast morning show. The host, Laurier LaPierre, thinks John was better off in the woods and thinks we should toss him back. Got my smallpox shot, discussed with the press bureau the plans for shipping out early film, tapes and blood; gobbled lunch. At 12:15 a prearranged recorded interview with Canadian Radio.

Our Monday lab meeting followed. Howard Poizner did a splendid job of summarizing the literature on cerebral dominance for language and described his forthcoming experiment to discover if the left half of the brain is dominant in processing sign language as it is in processing spoken language (in right-handed people). Reviewed some research proposals with Ivy, dropped off with the dean my request for a travel advance, and joined the tenure and promotion committee. Should a flautist be promoted for being a good flautist?

Called Father Sorelle again. He has cabled their representative in Burundi, Father Pagé, and is sending me via special delivery letters of introduction to the bishop of Bujumbura, Father Michel Ntuyahaga, and to the bishop of Gitega, Father Andrew Makarakiza—both black White Fathers, as he put it. Finally, chatted with Richard, who is learning the symptoms (and, I hope, the cures) of the top forty in tropical diseases.

PREPARATIONS

TUESDAY, MAY 18 — BOSTON

~~More radio interviews today. Then the Health Department down-~~ town stamped my smallpox certificate. Taught a class from one to four. Air France will give us VIP treatment, no doubt because our story was on Walter Cronkite's show. I checked on flights from Bujumbura to Europe to spirit out the blood, urine and films; the only direct flights are to Brussels on Sabena:

Mon. SN 498 lv 8:00 A.M. arr. 6:40 P.M. Mon.
Tues. SN 494 lv 6:40 P.M. arr. 6:05 A.M. Wed.
Thurs. SN 496 lv 8:00 A.M. arr. 7:00 P.M. Thurs.

The *Washington Post* just called; I have also had calls from representatives of *Time, Newsweek, Der Stern,* and *Die Welt,* who want serial rights. Harvard Press, Little, Brown and Addison-Wesley have also written or called about the book rights. We have put them all off until we return. The Grant Foundation telegraphed approval of our grant request today—$6,000 for travel, gift to the orphanage, and equipment. I guess we are really going.

WEDNESDAY, MAY 19 — BOSTON

Awoke frightfully early. Tempted to go in to the office but knew I'd be whipped later, so I took a pill. The cat woke me at ten. Still not possible to pick up the Grant money—two more vice-presidents need to sign. A round of interviews with radio stations, with Globe Communications and with *Time.* Tried to persuade AP Boston *not* to send in their Nairobi correspondent. Threatened noncooperation. Promised to send him a cable from Bujumbura on Monday the 31st.

Last year Richard asked me to give a talk on sign language to the psychiatrists at Boston University on May 19—today. Now he says the psychiatrists want to hear about Victor and John instead, so I set aside my prepared talk (carefully designed to be serious, scientific and over their heads) and narrated the tales of the two boys, complete with morals for the doctors to think about.

Next, I rushed to the WMEX talk show. The host, Avi Nelson,

reputed to be something of an ogre, turned out to be a delightful, effervescent young man with a sense of humor. I was queried by the public on B. F. Skinner's politics, the wisdom of capturing the boy in the first place, and whether we're using public funds. A thirteen-year-old called in with the two best questions. What will we do with John after we are through studying him? I replied that it depends on what's wrong with him. If he knows monkey language will it be harder to teach him human language? My answer was, no one knows, but probably.

Returned home to eat and pack. Frank, with whom I had shared everything the past dozen years, including our planning for Burundi, called off the checklist as Richard and I stowed the articles. Nine pieces of luggage in all!

Spent the evening reading some articles on the grey enkende and a stack of mail from people who had heard about our mission on radio and TV. First, about the monkeys: I learned from Chiarelli's *Atlas of Living Primates* that "enkende" (the term used in Barritt's article) is vernacular for *Cercopithecus lhoesti.* Napier and Napier's *Handbook of Living Primates* gives:

> Genus *Cercopithecus* (Linnaeus 1758)
> Nine species groups including *lhoesti*
> group with two species: *C. lhoesti* and
> *C. preussi.*

The genus *Cercopithecus* ("guenons"), the Napiers continue, is found in most of the rain forest, woodland and savannah of sub-Saharan Africa. *C. lhoesti* inhabits montane forest up to 8,000 feet but rarely higher. Consistent with this description of the guenon's habitat, Nyanza Lac, where Barritt says John was caught, is on the shores of Lake Tanganyika in the Imbo plains, with an elevation less than 3,500 feet. The region is part of the Great East Africa Rift Valley and contains many savannah animals. Along these plains extends a belt of foothills that contain gallery forests, in which tree branches tend to form canopies over open aisles, or galleries. So far so good. *C. lhoesti* eats leaves, green shoots, fruits and cultivated native crop plants. Correspondingly, the savannahs of western Burundi contain acacia and palm trees, thorny plants and grasses, as well as corn, rice and other crops.

PREPARATIONS

Guenons are diurnal; their principal feeding periods are early morning and evening. They are preyed upon by the eagle and the leopard. Guenons are quadruped but capable of climbing, jumping, running on the ground and crossing gaps in the jungle canopy by downward jumps. These observations check out, too, as Barritt talks of the enkendes scattering to the tops of nearby trees. All species have ischial callosities (that is, they have callused buttocks), which are believed to be associated with sitting and night-resting posture. When the guenon is threatened he lowers his head, raises his tail, holds his arms out stiffly, throws branches and whatever else he gets his hands on, defecates, urinates and vocalizes (not unlike the threat response of some university bureaucrats). According to the book, the species *C. lhoesti*, the enkendes, are found in Central and East Africa, including the lowland forests of Zaire and the western mountainous region of Uganda. Enkendes are both arboreal and ground-living. Their hair is long, soft, and dark grey, and they have a chestnut saddle. Their throats and chests are white; their remaining underparts, blackish brown. Thick grey tufts run upward and backward on the sides of their faces, and pale stripes run along under their eyes. I am not at all certain I could recognize one from the black-and-white photograph.

As to the stack of mail on my desk, some of it is from friends, enclosing clippings about our expedition from their local newspapers. The press bureau at Northeastern tells me they already have hundreds of clippings in their file. The intense public interest—television, radio, newspapers and the mail—cries out for some explanation. Why are we so fascinated by the idea of wild men? Some of the many letters in the stack give a clue. Several people urge us to leave the boy alone in the forest, or now that he has been cruelly captured, to put him back.

> Dr. Harlan Lane:
>   In the name of compassion for this unfortunate "Monkey boy" apparently raised by or associated with monkeys who cannot speak, but chatters in presumably monkey language, and refuses to wear clothes, we believe this boy should be RETURNED TO THE MONKEY AREA FROM WHENCE SOLDIERS CAPTURED HIM, and FORBID anyone to molest or take him away again.

And another letter, signed, I believe, by three students:

> Dear Sirs:
> We read the article about "John, your banana-loving boy" in the *San Francisco Chronicle* (5/14/76) and are very disturbed to hear about your rehabilitation program for a child who appears to be living in an environment suited to his needs. Science seems to have no place or understanding for this boy and we feel it is very inhumane to bring him back to a society based on our needs.
> Is it not possible to observe him in his environment? What are your motives for this "experiment"? Please send us any information.

A university professor wrote:

> Dear Dr. Lane:
> Recently, I read an article of interest in our local newspaper concerning a "wild boy" that was discovered living with monkeys in Africa. The article stated that you would travel to Africa to study the child and attempt to "rehabilitate" him. My concern is why you feel the child, after reportedly living in the jungle for four years, *needs* to be "rehabilitated." Why are "civilized" people always trying to "civilize" the "uncivilized"? Why do we feel civilization is so much better?
> As I see it, the child has adapted to the wild and the monkey way of life. He has never known anything different. It appears to me that the venture is merely an experiment. Are you considering the consequences of this venture? What will happen to the boy if "rehabilitation" is not a success? Will he be institutionalized, or caged might be a more descriptive word, as wild animals are in zoos? I must admit that it sounds like an interesting undertaking, but I strongly believe that there are some situations where man's meddling is more harmful than beneficial. Years from now, will you be able to live with the results if the experiment fails —will the child?

Some of the letters are from the lunatic fringe:

> Dear Dr. Lane:
> I am a wild person. I was never arrested and do not wish to be. I should like a list of foods I can eat to get my cool. Send it as soon as possible.

PREPARATIONS

Some send offers of help. A high school student in Norman, Oklahoma, is willing to come to Boston and take care of John if he returns with us. A woman in Leucadia, California, has been studying palmistry for six years and feels that "it is a beneficial and very valuable tool for character diagnosis. Send me a copy of his palm prints and I will return to you a thorough, complete character diagnosis of John."

I am saddened by the letters. What a grim commentary on our lives! Is life in the home sweet home so punitive that we prefer life in isolation, scrabbling for food, fleeing predators, neither giving nor receiving love? Are people fascinated by John because it appears that he had managed to escape what they cannot? Do they recognize, to their horror and fascination, the acting out of their own desires unbridled by social constraints? Perhaps the image of John's (or Victor's) life in union with nature calls to mind moments of their own past, moments full of freedom and serenity, moments in which they, too, communed with the universe. Wild children may be a reassuring witness that, no matter how utterly a child is rejected by its parents, there is a benign nature that looks after all its children. Finally, the letters, like the interest of the press, may reflect intellectual curiosity: with proper observation, John, like Victor, can clarify what is characteristic about man, his native endowment, and the relative importance of nature and nurture in his development. Some of these possible explanations are doubtful, but the timelessness of such speculations cannot be doubted. Romulus and Remus, the satyrs in Greek and Roman antiquity and the Middle Ages, wild children in the Renaissance, Robinson Crusoe, Mowgli, Tarzan—for that matter, King Kong—all cry out for an explanation. Perhaps John can help us to penetrate that mystery, too.

THURSDAY, MAY 20—EN ROUTE TO PARIS

Picked up traveler's checks, dry cleaning, baggage tags. At the office, wrote my last memos before leaving and proofread my report to President Ryder on the personalized system of instruction. The vice-president wants to see me when I get back about the position of acting dean (will he ask me if I want it or whom I want to see in it?). *Harper's* called to ask if I would do a story for them about John. Taught from one to four; the office staff had champagne ready and toasted our trip.

Final packing, a snack, and I dozed. Richard and his lover David arrived and we set off for Logan. At the airport we're pursued by press photographers, so we escape into the VIP lounge. David gave Richard a rose and a fond embrace. Several drinks, pictures, and hugs later, we're off. Four A.M.—what a ghastly hour to plan to arrive in Paris. Someday people won't believe what our generation went through to cross the Atlantic.

III

THE FRENCH CONNECTION

De Gaulle airport. Nine in the morning—four in the morning. Bleary-eyed. Hung over from the Seconal. The French understand: with eleven cases I wheel through the exit marked "Nothing to declare." Why must the Americans paw through every last piece of dirty underwear? Is our economy so much more fragile? Is it voyeurism?

Frank and I had lived in Paris for six years while I taught at the Sorbonne. Two friends from those days, Yvan and Christian, are at the airport to meet us, and we nestle in the back of Christian's Peugeot, bathed in Brahms and the scent of Gauloises, gazing out at the housing projects slipping by. In a moment we are wedged into a stream of traffic snaking its way through cobblestone streets. Two centuries in one glimpse: through the trees, a mansard roof, an ornately sculptured façade, a man leaning on the filigreed railing of a balcony, framed in stately French windows thrown open into an apartment behind; at his feet, white letters outlined in neon on a crimson field—*nettoyage à sec;* below, a plate-glass storefront, then steam rising from a manhole cover. The light changes. We gain on women carrying vegetables in net bags, an Arab trailing a twig broom in the gutter, a waiter in his white jacket and black mustache (both donned for the day?) rushing back inside his café for two more *express—deux—à la terrasse.*

Our hotel, The Sofitel Bourbon, is in a chic quarter of the Left Bank, on a narrow street bordered by palatial ministries, around the corner from the vast plaza of Les Invalides and just off the Place des Bourbons, a period piece, a miniature enclave of calm, imposing façades, art galleries and cafés. The hotel is small, elegant and redolent of money; we register in hushed tones. Richard wants to sleep, Yvan and I to catch up on lost time.

At Christian's that evening, a linguist friend showed us a cartoon about John the Jungle Boy that he had clipped from a Paris newspaper, a fortnightly satire called *Charlie Hebdo.* Christian's apartment, perched in the middle of the Seine on the Ile Saint-Louis, is modern and brightly colored but small and crowded with antique furniture. Over drinks, the best translation of the cartoon is disputed. In any case, John's fame is spreading.

Three French students stop by the apartment and the crowd migrates to Montparnasse and a small restaurant popular with performers and gays, Chez Maria, run by an American woman and her French husband. The kitchen is minuscule, the décor shabby, the fetid Turkish toilet is across the courtyard, and the food is superlative. At midnight, Adrien and Alain join our table of eight and the conversation takes a fresh start: Olivier (the doctor) wants to practice medicine in the States, Alain has no desire to go there but has an American client busted for drugs, Christian knows a restaurant with better *bifteck au Roquefort,* everyone knows a bit about Burundi, and no one is surprised that Americans do not; Olivier (the student) knows a joke about an elephant and a mouse, Adrien suggests we stop over in his native Ceylon—that sort of thing until 3:00 A.M. Yvan and I head back to the hotel while Richard sets out on foot along the boulevards, in pursuit of the crowds and bustle of the city that never sleeps.

THE FRENCH CONNECTION

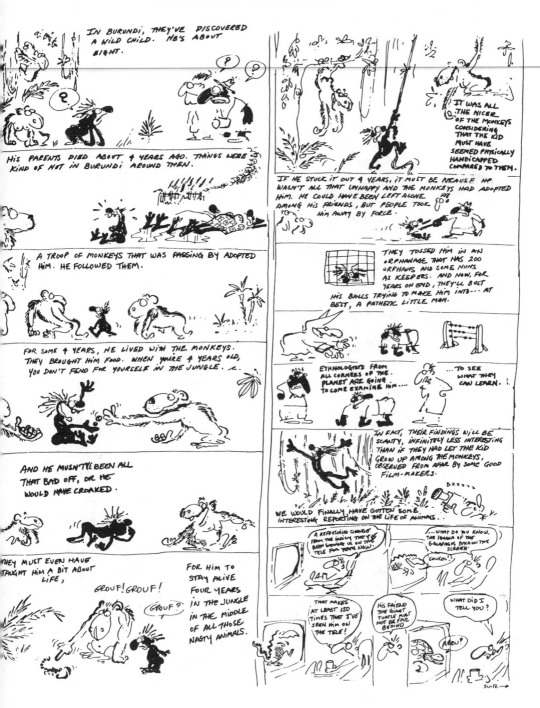

THE WILD BOY OF BURUNDI

THE FRENCH CONNECTION

SATURDAY, MAY 22—PARIS

We woke to a splendid, sunny day, the kind tourists dream about. Richard got me started on an account of Victor's arrival in Paris, more than a century and a half ago. My narrative began over coffee and continued as we strolled the Paris streets to visit the places themselves where Victor was housed, studied, and discussed.

When Victor was caught in the first days of 1800, word spread rapidly, and scholars in Paris were most anxious to get the boy to the capital before the yokels down south ruined this incredible experiment of nature. They wanted to observe his behavior before it lost some of its wildness through life in captivity. Observation was the watchword of the day, thanks to Condillac's empiricist philosophy, which had it that all knowledge came through the senses. In any case, just weeks before Victor had been captured, a group of scientists got together to form a kind of anthropological society, the first ever, called the Society of Observers of Man. There were some well-known names: Baron Georges Cuvier, who founded the fields of comparative anatomy and paleontology; Philippe Pinel, the first psychiatrist and the man who ordered the insane unchained; Abbé Sicard, a linguist and educator and head of the National Institution for Deaf-Mutes; and a naturalist named L.-F. Jauffret, who lived on the same street as our café, a little further down behind the Odéon, and who was the secretary of the society. Jauffret shot off a letter to the orphanage in Saint-Affrique, where Victor had been taken, instructing them to have the boy shipped to Paris at his expense, so Victor could be placed in Sicard's institute for observation and ultimately for instruction with other deaf-mutes. Recall that since Victor was mute, it was assumed that he was deaf.

But Victor's caretakers in Aveyron were not willing to have him moved. Bonnaterre wanted to study the boy in his school in the provincial capital, Rodez; he had written the section on zoology for a new edition of Diderot's *Encyclopédie,* so he reasoned that he knew how to study a wild child. Back in Paris, Sicard got very upset with the delay and went to see Napoleon's brother, Lucien Bonaparte, who was Minister of the Interior. He ordered the boy brought to Paris, and there was a great flurry of letters back and forth, but since it took five months before Victor finally left Aveyron, Bonnaterre was able to complete his studies and write his report. Bureaucracy hasn't really changed much. During the three-week trip north, Victor caught smallpox—his introduction to the advantages of life in society.

Richard and I left the café and walked down the rue de Vaugirard to the Luxembourg Palace, now the home of the French Senate, and we entered the spacious gardens by the main gate, opposite the teeming intersection where the rue Gay-Lussac and the boulevard Saint-Michel meet. Suddenly we felt becalmed; the din of traffic was muffled and I could hear children playing by the pond. We gazed out over the sprawling lawns bordered by hedges, gravel paths and statues, and I tried to make out the farthest limit, halfway to the observatory, but it was veiled in mist.

"When you get onto Victor there's no stopping you," Richard said. "I know why we're here in the Luxembourg Gardens; the first sentence of your book has Victor and Itard meeting right here."

"Right. This is where the morality play is staged. It is the summer of the year 1800. Enter right, Victor, the ultimate pupil, straight from the provinces. Not only is he ignorant of religion, morality, science, government, customs, clothing, and so on, but he is even ignorant of the means through which these could be taught to him—language. He is like the statue that Condillac asks us to imagine, which starts out *tabula rasa* and becomes a man by acquiring knowledge through the senses: he has to learn to see, to hear, to attend, to remember, to judge. Enter left, Jean-Marc Itard, the ultimate pedagogue: an inspired surgeon, a student of Pinel's, resident physician at Sicard's National Institution for Deaf-Mutes, an unflagging observer who for five long years would prove tireless and ingenious in devising techniques of instruction."

"I wonder what they thought of each other when they met."

"Itard wrote in his first report to the minister that he found Victor a filthy urchin, who swayed back and forth like a caged animal, who fixated on nothing and bit people who came too close. Whatever Rousseau may have thought, this savage was definitely not noble. Probably Itard expected as much; he deeply believed in Condillac and his premise that all knowledge comes through the senses—that's to say, through experience. Since Victor's experiences had been outside of society, he was not a social being. All that had to be done to rehabilitate him was to give him other experiences more suited to life in society."

"His growth had to be cultivated to society's design, like the gardens themselves. I can see why this view would be congenial to a behaviorist."

"I've a confession to make, Richard. My book has Victor and Itard meeting here, but that's poetic license. Truffaut, in his film, has them meeting at Sicard's institute, only a few streets from here, which is probably closer to the truth. Paintings of Victor and Itard survive, so Truffaut could re-create them rather accurately. The boy was twelve or thirteen and quite short even for that time—some four and a half feet. That's worth remembering, since John is supposed to be stunted. He had a light complexion and pockmarked skin, covered with scars—on the eyebrows, chin, cheeks. Like Itard, he had dark eyes, long eyelashes, a pointed nose. Unlike him, he had straight hair, a receding chin, a round face and—his most interesting feature—a huge scar across his larynx. The chances are that his throat was cut and he was abandoned for dead in the forest. Itard was about twice Victor's age and a bit of a dandy. He was born in Provence and had Mediterranean features— curly hair, a slanted forehead, an aquiline nose, a jutting chin. He wore a frilly shirt and a long coat drawn in at the waist with full lapels. Victor, by the way, wouldn't wear clothes at first; they fitted him with a kind of nightshirt and had to belt it on."

We crossed the Gardens and the boulevard Saint-Michel, turned right on the rue de l'Abbé de l'Epée and approached the National Institute for the Deaf. It is surrounded by high walls breached by a huge iron gate. Pedestrians were hurrying by the portals, obviously without any thought to all the historic events that had transpired on the other side. This was where the little community of deaf children brought together by Abbé Charles-Michel de l'Epée before the French Revolution was transplanted on his death. Here the growing community took root and flourished under his successor, Abbé Sicard. This is where sign language flourished and then spread through much of Europe and the United States, bringing with it the education of the deaf and their accession to full human rights. We slipped past an occupied concierge and entered a cobblestone courtyard bounded on three sides by the institute and its wings and containing a statue of Abbé de l'Epée in the center. As we entered the building and mounted the main staircase, I resumed my story.

"In his review of my book in the *Times*, Roger Shattuck contends that Victor was lodged and instructed here in an apartment on the upper floor. I have him living down the street in Itard's home. Just the sort of issue scholars tend to argue about. In any case, you get a good view of the institute gardens from here where Itard says Victor spent many a lonely moonlit night. Ironically, so did Itard. In his failing years, a bachelor suffering greatly from poor health, he had a thatched cottage constructed for himself in these gardens where he, too, would spend many solitary hours. This is the attic where Victor was placed when he arrived."

It was an ordinary enough attic under the eaves: rather dark and hot, dusty, and bare except for a few cardboard boxes. No trace of wild boys. The psychiatrist Pinel had rushed over here to see Victor before anyone else, but presently there was a long queue and Bonnaterre's gardener, who had accompanied Victor to Paris, would let people in to see the boy for a fee. One can easily understand how terribly important he was to people then, just as John is to us now. First he had general appeal; people of every walk of life read about him in the papers and came to see him for the same reasons that we in Boston were hounded by the press, the same reasons that people are always intrigued by wild men, by Romulus and Remus, by Mowgli, Tarzan and Robinson Crusoe. But Victor was an experiment of nature of specific interest to scholars such as Pinel because he was to resolve the major philosophical issues of the time. The most significant question was: What makes us human? Laymen and scholars alike were rather unsure how to circumscribe the family of man. In 1735, Linnaeus had published a tree of the animal kingdom in which men and monkeys were scandalously placed on the same branch. Making it even more difficult to draw the dividing line, societies like the Observers of Man had been sponsoring expeditions to Africa, India and the South Pacific that returned with a parade of Pygmies, gorillas, Hottentots and orangutans that made the rounds of the European capitals to the fascination of one and all. How could one decide if any of these creatures was truly human? An important question, for humans had souls to be saved and beasts did not. Upright posture first seemed a promising criterion, but it would not do. Orangutans, from the Malay words meaning "men of the forest," walked upright, whereas Victor had reportedly run on all fours while in Aveyron, suggesting that man would prove quadruped if society did not interfere. In fact, most Europeans saw little resemblance between themselves and any member of this bestiary and were prepared to exclude the whole lot from salvation. Well, there was always the criterion of language to separate man from beast. Except that Victor looked like a man but had no language. How could he be judged human while apes were not, if possessing language were the sole distinction?

"And, as it turns out, you can teach a chimp language," Richard interjected.

"They had even thought of that. The philosopher La Mettrie suggested trying to educate orangutans as we educate the deaf."

"Did they consider cross-breeding as a way of distinguishing humankind?"

"Believe it or not, they did propose mating an orangutan and a prostitute. Of course the clergy was outraged, which, as Rousseau pointed out, prejudged the question that the experiment was designed to answer."

"What strikes me is how up-to-date it all is," Richard said. "Is man different from the animals in having language? That's still a hotly disputed matter. Can humans learn animal communication and animals human language? Did John pick up the monkeylike chattering as a real communication system because he was reared by monkeys during a critical period in his development?"

"As if that weren't enough reason to send Pinel and his likes scurrying to see Victor, there was yet another question the boy might be able to clear up—namely, what does man owe to his nature and what to his nurture?"

"In other words," Richard said, "what is innate and what is acquired."

"Right. There is no thought without language, that's what Condillac said. So he believed that there are no innate ideas: deprive someone of language and his mind will be a void; he will be an idiot. Would Victor in fact resemble an idiot? Which of all our countless discriminations, concepts, tastes, skills, fears and desires would he lack and which would he prove to have natively, or in any event, without social intervention?"

"And of course we're asking the same questions of John. Will his gait, eye-hand coordination, depth perception, hearing, food preferences, affections, even his reflexes, be like those of a normal young boy in society? To that extent, they must be biologically predetermined, innate, environment-free. It looks like the opposite was closer to the truth in Victor's case, and from what we know of it, in John's."

"So Victor was to help resolve, first, the question of what it takes to be counted in the ranks of mankind and, second, how important it is to grow up in those ranks. He was also to help answer a third burning question: How perfectible is man?"

"The French Revolution brought many reforms based on the idea that man was perfectible—including the reform that created the National Institution for Deaf-Mutes. But wild children had always been an embarrassment, since they were not perfectible. You just couldn't educate them. Itard agreed to train Victor because Sicard asked him to, and because he thought it might bring him glory, but also because he deeply believed Condillac's view that man is what we make him. Itard thought he could prove this by socializing Victor."

"In that, you're like Itard."

"And you, *mon cher* Richard, are Pinel, the psychiatrist. He poked Victor here and there, observed him in that little attic, half-starved, half-crazed with fear, unkempt, mute, and he concluded that Victor's constitution was defective, that he was an idiot indistinguishable from

THE FRENCH CONNECTION

many of his charges at La Salpêtrière. Here, at the Sorbonne, is where Pinel addressed the Society of the Observers of Man."

~~We had turned off the Boul' Mich' and were crossing the Place~~ de la Sorbonne. We entered the ancient courtyard and made for the amphitheater.

I continued. "Victor is not an idiot because he was left in the wild, he was left in the wild because he was an idiot—that was Pinel's conclusion. But Victor was able to choose and prepare his own foods —shelling beans, for example. 'Merely automatic imitation,' says Pinel. He came to love Itard's housekeeper, Madame Guerin. 'A weak imitation of true sentiment.' He would put away food for another day. 'Purely animal instinct.' The same boy who clambered up trees and leapt from one to the next had, according to Pinel, poor eye-hand coordination. The child who, chez Bonnaterre, would fetch a shovel and give it to the gardener, signaling him to go for coal when the fire began to go out, could not, according to psychiatry's founding father, express himself by sound or gesture. Suppose Victor had taken Pinel forcibly into *his* environment and had examined his ability to spot predators, select foods, hear movement, climb trees and move his portly two-hundred-odd pounds through the brush—wouldn't he have concluded that Pinel was constitutionally defective and needed custodial care? God protect us from psychiatric diagnosis!"

"You mean from incorrect diagnosis, Harlan. We won't make the same mistakes with John. If he lived in the wild—and that's a big if —his adaptation to that milieu is every bit as real as ours to our own and he'll have a chance to show it, by his behavior, by his physical condition, by his body chemistry."

We sat down in the cavernous lecture hall and I tried to imagine Pinel on the stage intoning his harsh prognosis. Later I would look up his speech; this is how it concluded:

It has been necessary therefore to reconsider the present subject of research from another point of view or, rather, to undertake to verify the suspicions of imbecility that Bonnaterre had already formed concerning the child of Aveyron. . . . These suspicions could only be confirmed by attentive study to the customs and habits of this child at different times, and by disallowing any new development in intellectual faculties since his arrival in Paris. His outward actions, limited to a sort of animal instinct, gave us the idea of comparing him with children and adults whose intellectual faculties are more or less damaged and who, incapable of providing for their own subsistence, are confined in the state asylums. The history of several of them has brought out all the points of similarity that can exist. The objects of comparison are here before our very eyes, and each person can come to examine, study, observe the facts on which our account is based. Some of the children in our asylums reduced to a state of idiocy or insanity are inferior in intellectual faculties to the child of Aveyron, others are his equal or are even superior to him. Do we not then have every reason to think that the child of Aveyron ought to be considered in the same category with the children or adults fallen into insanity or idiocy? . . . Do these not assert that the child ought to be categorized among the children suffering from idiocy and insanity, and that there is no hope whatever of obtaining some measure of success through systematic and continued instruction?

"Since we are presuming to be the modern parallels of Itard and Pinel," Richard said, "let me argue Pinel's case for a moment. He clearly recognized that there were different degrees of retardation, and in at least a limited sense, he was correct in placing Victor's abilities within the retarded category. He also realized that the retarded kids in his institution learned very much more slowly than normal children, and there too he saw a parallel with Victor. Remember, Pinel was the first psychiatrist, not the latest, and I'm not so sure he was wrong about Victor."

"A lot of people would agree with you," I answered. "There are many who say that he was congenitally retarded, hence a poor test case for the question of how perfectible man is, of how much experience can mold and remold the normal human being. Claude Lévi-Strauss argues that, for one, and Maria Montessori, for another; also the developmental psychologist Arnold Gesell. And in Pinel's time, the famous phrenologist Franz Gall, and the surgeon-general of Napoleon's army, Baron Dominique Larrey, and the great naturalist of the day, Jean-Baptiste Bory de Saint-Vincent—all of these experts and more said

Victor was a congenital idiot. But they are wrong, and Pinel was wrong.
Pinel had no tools of analysis. He couldn't test Victor's blood for
phenylketonuria or any other congenital disease; he couldn't X-ray the
boy's skull for evidence of trauma or growths or malformations. He
couldn't even look at his vocal cords with a dental mirror to see if both
cords could still vibrate. All he could do was compare Victor against
a standard, an archetype of the category 'idiot,' and there he made
several fatal mistakes.

"First, he judged Victor from the doctor's vantage point and not
the patient's, so he missed all the things that Victor could do. For
example, Victor was incredibly agile, whereas a child so profoundly
retarded as to lack language would almost surely have motor problems.
Second, he judged Victor an idiot because the boy shared traits with
the children in La Salpêtrière; but who says they were idiots? Do you
know who landed there when Pinel was appointed chief physician in
the 1790's? Epileptics, albinos, the insane and the retarded. They
would spend a week or so at the Hôtel-Dieu—it's just down the Boul'
Mich' here, on the Ile de la Cité in the Seine—where they were bled,
and then they were sent to La Salpêtrière or Bicêtre, where they were
chained naked in rat-infested cubicles below ground, and fed bread and
soup. In comparing A and B, Pinel was on unsure footing both with
A and B."

"Listen, Harlan," Richard argued as we came out into the dazzling sunlight and headed down the rue de la Sorbonne, "what did you
expect him to do? He didn't have ways of measuring intelligence—his
compatriot Alfred Binet came up with IQ testing a century later—and
you criticize Pinel for lacking an IQ test free of cultural bias. Your
argument is: Victor could not be expected to do well on verbal reasoning and mathematical calculations, but give him a performance test like
food finding and he should do better than any idiot."

"Exactly. But Pinel's biggest mistake was his failure to realize that
the same effects can be produced by different causes. A child might not
use the toilet, for example, and thus foul his clothes because he is
retarded *or* because he has been living without clothes where there are
no toilets. Likewise, Victor's wandering gaze could have been a sign of

retardation, but it may have been a highly adaptive surveillance of the environment by a terrified creature."

We went down into the cool, dark Métro tunnel and found a train in the station. The gates to the platform were closed, so we had to wait.

"All in all, Richard, I believe that Victor began life as a normal child, that his is a story about human adaptiveness, not human frailty. You have to admire Itard, a twenty-six-year-old fresh from the provinces, standing up to all these luminaries—especially Pinel, his own teacher—and saying, 'No, the wild boy is just what he must be, given his experiences. I will educate him.' It's important to realize that idiocy was untreatable, idiots uneducable. I think Itard would see the reasons I have given you for believing Pinel was wrong, but there are two more reasons he couldn't see. By now we can count some three dozen wild children of record, aside from John. In every case the child is mute when captured. In every case of prolonged isolation, there is no recovery from mutism. In every case, vision, hearing and smell are acute in relation to food but bizarre in relation to other stimuli. Many of the children are insensitive to heat and cold; most shun society and seek to escape. Most walk occasionally on their hands and feet. Now all of this fits Victor to a tee and was the basis of Pinel's diagnosis, so you would have to conclude that all thirty-five other children were brain-damaged from birth—not very likely. And, before you accuse me of beating a dead horse, think about this. You have to be pretty severely brain-damaged not to start acquiring speech by the age of, say, two. How could three dozen children, all profoundly brain-damaged, fend for themselves successfully in the forest, some of them as young as five or six years old, like Victor?"

"I'm a professional skeptic, Harlan! In any case, the differential diagnosis ought to be easier with John. In the century and a half since Pinel we've identified dozens of physiological causes of mental retardation, and we can check them off one by one. If any one of them fits, that's probably the end of the story. We can also try to find John's parents and run down his life, and if there are no substantial gaps, we can end the story that way. One final defense of Pinel—we should examine the piece of evidence he would probably want to stake his case on: if Victor was not retarded, how do you explain the slowness with which he acquired the behavior of a civilized Frenchman? Take the deaf man Jean Massieu, whose eloquent petition to the government during the French Revolution saved Abbé Sicard's life. Before Sicard's school was founded, deaf children were regarded as brutes or idiots. But when they had the chance to acquire a communal language back there at Sicard's school, and to receive instruction in that language, they learned as rapidly as anyone else. Massieu said that without Sicard they would have been like animals. Now if only Victor had. written an eloquent testimonial to Itard, the matter of his native intelligence would be settled. That is exactly what everyone was hoping for from Victor's training."

"That and a first-hand account of life in the wild. Well, Victor made a lot of progress in five years. Intellectually, he learned to read and write in a modest way, according to Itard's reports. Socially, he became affectionate; took pride in the things he could do well; learned shame, outrage and remorse. But I think that for a long time he would have preferred the forests. I love the story about Madame Récamier inviting Itard and Victor to her château; since all Paris was talking about him, it really was a coup. I am still talking about the perfectibility of man, as you'll see. Madame Récamier had one of the great salons of the day, and members of the English Parliament and of the French government, actors, poets, scientists—even a future king, Bernadotte —were assembled for dinner. Victor was placed next to the hostess, presumably to show that even a child of nature would be dazzled by her beauty. His education had advanced far enough that he wore clothes, took his place and waited to be served. But after gorging himself with his hands, he slipped out, during a discussion of Voltaire's atheism, tore off his clothes, climbed a tree and leapt from one tree to the next, stark naked, the length of the avenue that approached the château. The women gaped and fanned themselves, the men urged all to stand back, the gardener tempted Victor down with fruit, and someone lamented that Rousseau could not live to see this proof that society is kinder to man than nature is."

"A good story," Richard said, "but the fact remains that Itard himself felt a sense of failure with Victor; the boy never really became civilized and was in custodial care with Itard's housekeeper until he died at forty."

"True, we have to provide an answer to the question of why Victor didn't go on to become, say, a professor and write an account of his life in the wild. Do you want Itard's answer? He concluded, like many psychologists nowadays, that there is a critical period of language learning and also cognitive development which had ended by the time he went to work with Victor. And, for safe measure, he threw in that prolonged isolation may have irreversible effects. He might well be right. And I'll add that Itard was a genius, but that his educational methods had some big flaws. To his credit, Itard was the first to see the pupil not as a little adult but as a developing child. He taught things in an order and at a variable rate tailored to the individual child's progress. He devised the first systematic method of teaching reading. He was the first inventor of instructional devices. He was enormously patient in proceeding by small steps. He was sharp at analyzing complex performances into their component skills. He understood the necessity for building on Victor's current needs and for giving him new needs, for the most part social. Yet he made mistakes. He isolated Victor from other children. Itard deprived Victor of all forms of sexual expression, yet was horrified at his growing sexuality. In short, he drew Victor back into a cocoon where life alternated between the house and the classroom in a highly planned way. What would Victor have become if, like Massieu, he had been taught sign language and allowed free commerce with the signing community that surrounded him? Perhaps, like Massieu, he would have become a teacher, or perhaps an architect, or a sculptor as did some of Massieu's classmates."

"If Itard's efforts with Victor were blocked because the boy had already passed through the critical period for language learning, then ours with John may be blocked, too; but if his failure was a matter of instructional technique—we'll see."

Sometime back we had taken a bus and made our way to the Bicêtre hospital. I guided Richard across the spacious grounds as I spoke. "In any case, Victor remained Victor and Itard went on to

THE FRENCH CONNECTION

other things. He founded modern otology, wrote the first textbook on diseases of the ear. He had a very successful private practice but he remained physician to the Institution for Deaf-Mutes. As he was dying, one of his students, Edward Seguin, proposed to train an idiot using the methods Itard had invented for Victor. I remember finding that the dictionary of medicine for that year said there was no treatment for idiocy, since to combat it you would have to change the brain and that was beyond reach. Anyway, Seguin, twenty-five, thought he'd like to try. A year later, Itard died and Seguin published. He had considerable success, had taught an idiot to read, to count and so on, and you can believe that caused quite a stir. He was invited to do a large-scale tryout with some idiots at La Salpêtrière, and when that worked, the government founded a school for him here at Bicêtre. Word spread throughout Europe and across the Atlantic, and George Sumner came to this very room to see the training method. In many ways it was a repeat of what Itard had done with Victor, although there was much more time and equipment devoted to motor skills, since idiots, unlike Victor, have motor problems. Sumner was so impressed that he got the Massachusetts legislature to found the first school for the retarded in the United States. It was called the State School for Idiotic Children, located in Boston, and the principal was sent over here to learn Seguin's methods. The method spread throughout Europe and the United States. Seguin went to America in his later years and founded several more schools for the retarded. Later, the original U.S. school moved to Waltham and changed its name to the Walter E. Fernald State School, where we've arranged to lodge John if we bring him back."

In the main corridor of the hospital, we followed the signs to the museum and entered a small room lined with glass cases containing some of Seguin's original instructional devices. A form board, perhaps the first ever. Blocks that look like dominoes and were used for building and combining. And a little frame that once had cloth flaps that the children learned to button and unbutton. It reminded Richard of his daughter's Montessori school—as well it should. Montessori had read Itard's two reports on Victor as well as Seguin's book on the training of idiots. It occurred to her that the same method of sensory education could be used with ordinary preschool children. She says modestly that she owes it all to Itard, but her method relies partly on the child's ability to teach himself, a luxury Itard couldn't afford with Victor.

The Montessori method is, however, guided by perhaps a half-dozen principles of education that Itard's experiment with Victor did indeed inspire. The first affirms the biological programming of child development, the child's capacity for self-realization, for "auto-education." The second calls for "scientific pedagogy," a science of childhood based on observation. The third demands a natural environment in which self-development can be expressed and observed. Montessori believed that the school could be made into such an environment, thus becoming a laboratory for scientific pedagogy. This environment should be determined scientifically. "In order to expand, the child, left at liberty to exercise his activities, ought to find in his surroundings something organized in direct relation to his internal organization." All of these principles imply the next, which Montessori calls the "biological concept of liberty in pedagogy": the child must be free to act spontaneously and to interact with the prepared environment. The entire program is concerned with the individual child; the spontaneity, the needs, the observation, the freedom are always those of the individual. Finally, the *modus operandi* of the method is sensory training.

In reviewing these six principles of the Montessori method, one can see how much it echoes Itard's. It was Itard who first broke with traditional subject-matter instruction and implemented the education of the individual child through interaction with a carefully prepared environment. It was Itard who first called for a scientific pedagogy based on philosophy and medicine, employing the technique of observation with which *Idéologie* had endowed these two disciplines. It was Itard who spent long hours watching for the spontaneous expressions of his pupil in nature as in society, and he who, following the precepts of mental medicine, tailored the child's environment to accommodate and shape his needs. And it was Itard who took Condillac's model of the development of the intellect and first created a program of sensory education.

THE FRENCH CONNECTION

In practice as in theory, Montessori's methods are, to a large extent, elaborations of those employed with Victor. The greater part of her program is concerned with education of the senses, and most of her considerable array of didactic materials is devoted to this purpose. There are twenty-six sets of apparatus that provide for training all the senses except taste and smell. Many of the devices are based on those originated by Seguin; others come from Itard, such as the drum and bell employed for training hearing or the geometric cutouts for vision. In every case, Itard's method of dwindling contrasts is employed. The program designed to enhance muscular coordination of the limbs and the devices for training manual skills owe much to Seguin. Montessori credits Itard with showing how perceptions and language can be associated, and she quotes at length from his description of these experiments with Victor.

Montessori schools, the education of the retarded, instructional devices—we owe all that to Victor and Itard. And what about John: what new impetus to education will he give? I wondered.

As we left the hospital grounds, we came abreast of four young men busily communicating with each other in signs. I mustered my courage, stopped them, and tried some sentences in American Sign Language, but as I expected, they understood not a word. (Although the sign language of the American Deaf was at one time very much like that of the French Deaf, since it was brought to America and disseminated by Abbé Sicard's deaf pupil Laurent Clerc, it has evolved separately over a century and a half and no longer resembles its parent.) I finally resorted to finger-spelling French, which was sufficient to exchange a few pleasantries. The hour was late and we returned to the hotel to change for dinner.

In the evening, Yvan drove Richard, Christian, and me chez Roland, who is well known for throwing great bashes.

At the party, Henri Sarlin, a Finnish friend, told us a fascinating story. Children are often lost in the scrub forests of Finland. Occasionally the National Guard has to go looking for them. The soldiers are taught that the lost child will not come to their call. They must search carefully for him, meter by meter, and must expect that, even if they spot him, he may run in fear. Is it possible, I wondered, that for some children the transition to a wild and suspicious state begins within hours of their separation from civilization? Perhaps survival is possible only for those who are able to make so quick an adaptation.

SUNDAY, MAY 23—PARIS
From Richard's diary

One of the comforts of the Sofitel Bourbon is that the draperies seal with Velcro around the edges so that no ray of morning sun will disturb the sleeper. We managed to get up eventually and make our way to the Champs-Elysées feeling exposed in the brilliant noonday sun. At breakfast Harlan had an inspiration. He knew the perfect country inn for lunch.

We left Paris with Yvan at the wheel heading generally east. After about thirty kilometers and a few turns we found a sign announcing the Auberge de La Dauberie near the village of Les Mousseaux. Imagine those beautiful French country inns pictured in *Gourmet* magazine —the Dauberie is still more beautiful. The main building is stone-roofed with heavy thatch. The tiled dining room leads in back to a small lawn set with umbrella-shaded tables where a crowd was dining. The hostess told us there would be a half-hour wait, gave us a menu and invited us to enjoy one of the handsomest country gardens I've ever seen. Beyond the dining area, late spring flowers of many kinds were blooming along with trees and shrubs. The arrangement was informal but certainly must keep several gardeners busy. I lay on the thick grass looking up through birch branches at the dazzling French sky. With my two friends, ready for a good lunch, in perfect health and anticipating our expedition, I wondered if my life would ever have a more perfect moment.

"Harlan, tell me again why Victor wasn't autistic. I'm lying here with my mind idling and I'm thinking of all the symptoms he had which fit that diagnosis. He's socially withdrawn, surely. He shows some measure of intelligence and motor skill while presenting sensory anomalies: hears some things and not others, is indifferent to temperature, has a wandering gaze. He's emotionally labile and preoccupied with order. Most important, he was mute."

"Finally, the diagnosis won't stick. First, Victor wasn't living autistically—that is to say, solely in his own community. He was a participating member of the community he was placed in, one that Itard inexcusably kept very small. Victor loved Madame Guerin and helped her with the housework; he cared for Itard, as he had for Bonnaterre before him, and took lessons from him daily. He went after the daughter of Itard's friend and cuddled with her in the Luxembourg Gardens. What you call emotional lability, I would call normal expressions of grief, anger, frustration—always appropriate to the situation. As for the fact that he kept his room tidy or liked to shell beans, I hardly think that makes him autistic. Perhaps they overdid his toilet training in Rodez, or perhaps Madame Guerin insisted on a tidy household. It's true that Victor had a high tolerance for cold, but my God, he had lived in the mountains unclad. Moreover, what are the chances that he could have survived there from age five, say, if he was so intellectually and emotionally disturbed he couldn't speak? We know that isolation alone will produce the mutism, so why must you add autism? Think about this: what is there about Victor's deviant behavior in society that cannot be explained by his adaptive behavior in the forest? Nothing.

"I suppose I sound a little dogmatic, Richard, but I'm rather disgusted with the psychoanalytic types who slapped that label on Victor for their own purposes. Bruno Bettelheim was the first, back in 1959. He had spent much of his career working with autistic children and was convinced that autism is caused by extreme emotional isolation, so Victor *had* to be autistic. Nowadays that theory of autism is still popular on the continent but is pretty much discredited in the United States and England. As Lorna Wing writes from London in her recent book on autism, well-controlled studies have failed to show any specific abnormalities of personality or of child rearing practices among groups of parents of autistic children. But Wing still wants Victor for her own and called my book about him "frustrating" because I failed to see how autistic he really was. For Wing, Victor was born autistic or became so following some childhood disease, although Bettelheim asserts that an autistic child could not long survive in the wild. To avoid all this confusion with John, we had better be prepared to document his case in far greater detail than could be done with Victor."

Eventually, lunch was served at the Dauberie: a delicate bouquet of flavors flawlessly presented. It did not seem much later that we were back at Christian and Henri's grappling with the choice of a restaurant for dinner; one was selected that was right on the Place de la Concorde. At dinner Henri had some news for us. A friend in Stockholm to whom he had mentioned our expedition had sent him a clipping from the Swedish newspaper *Kvällsposten*—an account of John! There were three pictures and a text Henri translated.

> A little girl led John up to us by the hand. He walked quite normally but kept his head down. Not a sound was coming from his lips. He was staring into nowhere and hit himself now and then on the forehead or over the shoulder as if he wanted to chase away some mosquitoes. This is how he looked: the boy who until a few months ago had lived among monkeys.

"Who wrote this?" we demanded. Did Barritt simply sell the article to another paper?

"It is signed just 'the reporter from *Kvällsposten*,' " said Henri, "but the author is a woman, listen to this:

> My husband, David, and I will never forget this hot Wednesday afternoon in December. The first thing I saw was the swollen stomach of the boy, a normal symptom of undernourished children in Africa. David grew up in Kenya with pet monkeys. He had not noticed the boy entering. All of a sudden he felt someone take his hand in a way which he afterwards described as identical to the way his monkeys used to do at home.

There followed some description of Burundi and of how the travelers found their way to Gitega. Some comments by Father Tuhabonye, then the description of John:

> The monkey boy kept completely quiet. I could not see any trembling or any other signs of fear, but this must have been what he felt because

he immediately started to defecate. . . . Sometimes he is much happier, said Father Pierre, but we doubt that he makes any progress. He has grown since he came here but we can't get his stomach to function properly. Maybe it is the human diet he cannot take after having eaten roots and fruits. . . . I was looking at John's skin and saw that it was very coarse on his arms and hands and almost worn off behind his ears. Again, signs of undernourishment. . . . David gave the monkey boy his shining ballpoint pen, but he threw it away without even playing with it. . . .

The article ended with the usual questions:

> . . . Had he been brain damaged from his birth and would that explain his behavior? . . . Did his parents die, or did they leave him and did they put him out in the forest? I would also like to know more about his behavior when the soldiers took care of him. . . .

We agreed there was nothing here that we didn't already know, but at least someone else had seen him and had described the circumstances roughly as Barritt had.

Night does not come to Paris until after ten at this time of year, for the capital is as far north as the northern tip of Maine. As dusk fell abruptly, all dinner conversation hushed and the majestic *Place* exploded into blazing light.

MONDAY, MAY 24—PARIS
From Richard's diary

Met Harlan and a friend, Nyoko, at the Deux Magots and we drove through the desperately crowded little streets of the old Jewish quarter to visit Nyoko's anthropologist friend, Pierre Smith. He is a chubby man about forty with a Rwandan wife, a new son and a formidable capacity for Scotch. Mme. Smith is the tallest, thinnest woman I have ever met, and is among the most handsome and charming.

Smith knew Rwanda better than Burundi, but he could give us some background. The Batutsi, nomadic herdsmen and warriors, migrated from the Nile area into the lake region of Central Africa between three and four hundred years ago. In what are now Rwanda and

Burundi they found the Bahutu, a sedentary, agricultural Bantu people. Not only did the tall and graceful Batutsi look upon all forms of manual labor with contempt, they regarded the stocky and short Bahutu as their natural inferiors on all counts. The Bahutu became vassals in their own land. They cultivated it as serfs, keeping a share of the produce and giving a portion to their Tutsi lords. The Bahutu were granted the privilege of caring for the Batutsi's treasured longhorn cattle. Use of the land, at least theoretically, belonged to the Tutsi mwami (king) who parceled it out to the ganwa (princes of royal blood), and to his chiefs and subchiefs, who in turn subdivided it among their kin.

As Pierre was speaking, I wondered how the Tutsi managed this political takeover without military conflict. After all, the Bahutu outnumber them even now by seven to one; why didn't they put up a fight? Part of the reason may have been military hardware. The pictures I had seen of Batutsi showed them dressed as warriors, holding slender crafted spears. As nomads and hunters, they must have been skillful with the weapons of the day. Perhaps they were also more nimble-minded or had developed a superior sense of political organization. It was easy to imagine symbolic reasons too as I watched the poised and graceful Mme. Smith. Perhaps the Bahutu came to share the Tutsi feeling for cattle as mythic symbols of life and wealth. I wasn't able to ask Pierre about this; he was totally absorbed in his narrative.

German colonial rule from 1885 to 1918 strengthened the position of the mwami but achieved little else. The Belgians, who administered the territory under a League of Nations mandate and then a United Nations trusteeship (1919–1962), chose, like the Germans, to do so through the mwami and the ganwa, Belgium's main colonial interest being the Congo (Zaire). It wasn't until 1955 that the feudal land-tenure system was abolished—and then only theoretically, for proposals to implement the change were never written into law. But the traditional social structure, particularly the relationship between Tutsi shebuja (lord) and Hutu mugabire (serf), began to weaken with the conversion to Christianity of a large sector of the population. There were sporadic revolts and in 1959 a serious outbreak of violence.

Burundi and Rwanda shared a common currency and an economic union under Belgian rule. These arrangements fell apart after independence as a Hutu government came to power in Rwanda and thousands of Batutsi took refuge in Burundi. In Burundi itself, Prince Louis Rwagasore tried to bridge ethnic differences with a broad-based anti-Belgian nationalist movement. Elected prime minister in 1961, Rwagasore was assassinated by Tutsi rivals a month after he took office. His successors have been unable to unite Bahutu and Batutsi, or to stay in power without recourse to violence. The prestige of Rwagasore's father, the elderly Mwami Mwambutsa IV, proved equally unavailing. The mwami was deposed in 1966, and a military republic was instituted that year under President Michel Micombero, then a twenty-six-year-old Tutsi army officer.

During his ten-year rule, Micombero tried but failed to resolve Burundi's ethnic conflict. Several limited Hutu uprisings were crushed, but in April 1972 a Hutu-led insurrection caused the death of hundreds of Batutsi and provoked widespread devastating reprisals. Educated Bahutu by the tens of thousands were systematically hunted down and killed. Also slain was the ex-mwami's son and heir, Ntare V, who had reigned for two months in 1966 and had recently returned to Burundi from exile.

The magnitude of this conflict was a crucial issue to us, since according to Barritt, John had lost his parents during it, and we pressed Pierre for details. A cloud of pain seemed to pass over his face as he spoke. The terror in Burundi during May and June of 1972 was a devastating human catastrophe. In the first stage of the rebellion, Bahutu were joined by Mulelists, a group of fanatics who use drugs and believe that certain magic phrases made them invulnerable to bullets. Their trainers would shoot blanks at them to convince the Mulelists of their invulnerability—then would shoot real bullets at a dog or cat to show that they were not protected without the magic phrases. The rebels' weapons were more often spears and machetes than guns, but with these they overran the provincial capitals of Rumonge and Nyanza Lac, Pierre told us. Several thousand Tutsi were killed and some horribly mutilated, most of them in the Bururi provinces where John was found. The counter-insurrection by the Tutsi army forces was even more terrible, and naturally the southern region where the uprisings had started felt the worst reprisals, Pierre said. It is easy to believe from the reports that a terrified child could have fled into the countryside, and if he survived, could have lived wild for a long period of time.

Located in the rugged mountains and craters north and east of Lake Tanganyika, the two peoples, Batutsi and Bahutu, share one language and many customs in the tiny, densely populated republic. Yet the Batutsi remain the masters, exploiting the Hutu majority much as they did for centuries under the Tutsi monarchy. Only 14 percent of the Burundi population, the Tutsi aristocracy relies on coercion to stay in power. They are all the more apprehensive in view of neighboring Rwanda's 1959 revolution, which ended Tutsi mastery in a similar set of circumstances, putting the Hutu into major control. The stark poverty of an economy based on coffee, cotton and little else feeds the fires of ethnic bitterness; Burundi is one of the poorest countries in the world.

Pierre is convinced that sooner or later, as in Rwanda, the Hutu majority will seize power. But the present government is determined to keep this from happening. The constant tension and prospects of violence keep most travelers away. "You must never say anything even remotely political while in Burundi," he warned us. "To do so could lead to immediate expulsion, or worse."

As four o'clock neared, we thanked the Smiths and Nyoko for their help, rejoined Yvan at the Sofitel Bourbon, and checked out. By five we were off for Brussels, where Sabena provides the major jet service to Bujumbura.

IV

BUJUMBURA

At the airport Richard and I met the usual international nuisances: buildings under construction, no place to park, hassles at the check-in counter. Our baggage is overweight—five hundred dollars' worth. I spoke with the stationmaster and finally persuaded him to waive the charges (only to recall later that we were saving CBS' money, not our own, but that will lessen my guilt if we can't get film out or if there is no story for CBS to tell).

We wondered how Sabena fills two jets a week to Bujumbura and Kigali. The answer is—with freight. Two-thirds of the plane is partitioned off for cargo (forward, so a sudden taxi stop won't slam it through the passengers) and the small seating space is completely full —with diplomats, students, businessmen and missionaries. Richard and I got into a discussion about some points of psychology and lan-

guage, designed the critical experiment to resolve our differences, and
—at two in the morning—tried to sleep. We failed. The cold and the
cramped seats taught us the true meaning of *Sabena:* Such a Bad
Experience, Never Again. Instead, we talked. Richard wanted to know
more about wild boys other than Victor. Unfortunately, there have
been very few: if you try to keep fact separate from fiction, you can't
go very far back in time; Victor is the only well-documented and
indisputable case.

In his *Discourses* Rousseau cites four cases. The wolf child of
Hesse was seven years old when discovered in 1344. After four years
in the forests, he could leap and run on all fours and was purportedly
protected by wolves. The bear child of Lithuania was found in 1694,
at the age of ten. He learned to walk upright and even to speak.
Condillac cites this case in support of his theory that there is no
memory without language. "The boy gave no sign of reason," Condillac
wrote. "He walked on all fours, had no language, uttered sounds that
were quite inhuman. It took a long time before he was able to say a
few words, and even then they were rather unformed. As soon as he
could speak, he was asked about his original condition, but he remembered no more of that than we remember of what happened to us in
the crib." (Four other wild children preceding this case are mentioned
by various other writers.) Next, Rousseau discusses a pair of children
who were lost in the Pyrenees and found in 1719. Peter of Hanover,
the last case Rousseau describes, is perhaps the twelfth wild child on
record and the first whose sketch has a fair amount of detail. He was
found in 1724, when he was thirteen years old, and he was still alive
when Rousseau wrote about him. He was reportedly found in the
forests, where he had been abandoned by his father, living on vegetables and bark. He despised captivity and succeeded in escaping several
times. He eventually learned to wear clothes but not to speak. Linnaeus
takes up these four cases and three others in discussing the species
Homo ferus.

Mlle. Le Blanc, from Sogny, in the Champagne region of France,
was the next famous case. When she was caught in the woods in 1731,
she was wearing animal skins and had scampered up a tree. She could

BUJUMBURA

swim and run, reports have it, preferred to drink rabbit blood and to eat frogs, fish and fowl. She later acquired language and could answer the burning question that the queen of Poland and the duke of Orleans came to put to her: did she have an idea of the Supreme Being before she learned to speak? She didn't at first, but had acquired one rapidly —no doubt assisted by the nuns responsible for her care. She revealed that she'd had a companion in the forests whom she had killed by accident.

There's an additional case, a girl who was lost in a snowstorm at age eight. She was known to have been a normally developed child and was recognized by her former schoolmates when she was found at age sixteen. This case was reported shortly before Victor's discovery in a book on timber exploitation in the Pyrenees, written by J. J. B. Leroy, a naval engineer responsible for obtaining masts for the French fleet. Leroy wrote:

> The forest here was so extensive and dense before we began to exploit it for timber some thirty years ago that a young wild girl, sixteen or seventeen years old, had lived in these woods some seven or eight years before capture. She had been left behind by a band of young girls who had been caught in the snow and who were forced to spend the night in these woods. The next day they looked at length for their friend without success and finally gave up. The girl, caught subsequently by farmers, remembered nothing of all this, had lost the use of speech, and would eat only plants. She was taken to the orphanage in the village of Moleon where she lived for many years, overwhelmed by melancholy, yearning for freedom, never speaking, and remaining almost immobile all day long, her head in her hands. She was of average build and had a rather hard look about her.

When Bonnaterre undertook to describe Victor, a score of years later, he cited all the previous cases, save the last. Like the boy of Lithuania, he said, Victor had nice features, fair skin, and slight build, no liking for ordinary foods, no speech; he seemed slow-witted and often tried to bite people. Like the boy from Hanover, Victor was covered with scars, selected his foods by smell, was mute, and could be gentle if caressed. Like the girl from Sogny, he drank prone from streams. Another of Victor's biographers (a schoolmate of Itard's who became a naturalist) said the boy had ten characteristics in common with other wild children: scars, leanness, sensitive hearing, mutism, guttural sounds, frightened look, eats raw meat, detests children, walks on all fours, climbs trees. Nine out of ten also apply to John, according to Barritt's article.

Between Victor of Aveyron and John of Burundi there are maybe three dozen more cases, of which the best known are Kaspar Hauser and Amala and Kamala of Midnapore. Hauser was seventeen when found in the town square of Nuremberg, apparently abandoned by his mother. He was mentally retarded. His case attracted a lot of notoriety, in part because of the progress he made in training, in part because of two attempts on his life, the second successful, and in part because of a rumor that he was sequestered and finally murdered, as he was in line to the French throne. In any case, there was never any reason to believe he had lived in the wild. Amala and Kamala, on the other hand, who were two and eight years old when found by the Reverend Singh in 1920, were discovered walking on all fours in the company of wolves. According to Singh, they had thick calluses on their palms, knees and elbows. Their tongues hung out of their mouths and their breathing recalled the panting of wolves. They detested light, sought to escape, ate only meat. Amala died after a year in captivity, Kamala eight years later—both apparently from kidney disease. After years of training, Kamala did learn to speak.

"You can't give much weight to the reports about any one of these wild children," Richard said. "But certain themes keep cropping up. Mutism and walking on all fours, both of which apparently apply to John. Then there's general insensitivity, especially to heat and cold, with the exception of anything having to do with food. All the children try to escape, and they shun humans. With training, some learn language and some don't."

"Well, I think there's a principle there," I answered. "Most wild children never learn to speak. The two exceptions are Mlle. Le Blanc and Kamala, and they both had companions in the wild."

BUJUMBURA

"You mean most wild children never *relearn* to speak," Richard objected. "They must have had language when they went into the wild —any child old enough and smart enough to fend for himself in the woods must have previously learned language in his home. I'm impressed again by what Henri told us in Paris about the Finns' experience hunting for lost children. Being lost and isolated must be an incredibly stressful experience that only a very few survive at all. Those who do probably undergo some pretty significant metabolic changes to adapt to their new habitat. Language is obviously a highly evolved ability, and I wonder if it isn't in a sense quite fragile—quickly lost in the face of severe stress and lack of social reinforcement and permanently lost if the isolation is prolonged."

"I think that's right. How can you explain the permanent mutism of all these wild children otherwise?"

"Do we know anything about adults in these circumstances? Prisoners who spend years in solitary confinement or shipwrecked sailors, for example?"

I told Richard about the famous case of the Scottish sailor Alexander Selkirk. He was born in 1676 in Largo, a fishing and shipping port. In 1703 he shipped out as sailing master on a privateer, the *Cinque Ports,* that plied the trade routes off the northwest coast of South America. A year later the ship put in to the island of Juan Fernández, in Chilean waters, for supplies and repairs and Selkirk demanded to be put ashore. He was counting on most of the men to join him, since they had recently threatened a mutiny, but the promise of booty dissuaded them and the captain marooned Selkirk alone. He was landed with a sea chest, a musket and ammunition. In the chest were clothes, the mathematical instruments of a sailing master, a Bible and other books, a kettle, a knife, a hatchet, and some unspecified "practical pieces." Selkirk's first fear was solitude; he was dejected, he later reported, and for eighteen months of isolation, he exerted himself as little as possible, but read his Bible and prayed. In the beginning, he lived in a small cave; later he built a little shelter out of stones.

Four years and four months after his abandonment, Selkirk was found by a landing party from the privateers *Duke* and *Duchess.* He fetched the sailors fresh water and crawfish and invited them to eat a stew of goat flesh he had prepared. Then he ran off and caught a goat. According to the captain, Woodes Rogers, Selkirk was wild-looking and covered in goatskins. He had built two huts with wood from pimento trees and had lined them with goatskins; he slept in one and "dressed his victuals" in the other. He kept himself occupied by reading, singing psalms and praying. He was barefoot and ran at great speed. He was much harassed at first by cats and rats, which, coming originally from ships that had revictualed there, had multiplied profusely. So he tamed some cats to protect him from the rats, and he tamed some kids.

Now the most important part. Here's what Rogers wrote in his diary: "At first coming on board us, he had so much forgot his language for want of use that we could scarce understand him, for he seemed to speak his words by halves. We offered him a dram, but he would not touch it, having drank nothing but water since his being there, and 'twas some time before he could relish our victuals." Rogers diary was published, making Selkirk famous, and Daniel Defoe and Sir Richard Steele, among others, interviewed him at length when he returned to England. Defoe based *Robinson Crusoe* on Selkirk's adventure. It was Rousseau's first reading assignment to his fictional pupil Emile. According to Steele, Selkirk was sociable but distracted. He got into a drunken brawl, married, joined the navy and died off the Gold Coast of yellow fever. In one interview he told Steele that on Juan Fernández he had formed a habit of using fixed times and places for prayers which he recited aloud "in order to keep up the facilities of speech and to utter himself with greater energy."

"So you think that if Selkirk hadn't had a Bible or other book," Richard mused, "or if the *Duke* and *Duchess* had arrived a year later, Rogers would have found a wild man who spoke not at all, instead of by halves."

"And no doubt prolonged isolation has more devastating and permanent effects on language when it occurs earlier in a person's life. All of the wild children were cut off from society before they had reached adolescence."

"Which means that if John has really lost his language from life

‡ 77 ‡

BUJUMBURA

in the wild, we may not be able to help him regain it."

"I don't know, Richard. There are three things in our—his—favor. He's still young. He may have been communicating with monkeys during his isolation, and communication apparently helped Mlle. Le Blanc and Kamala. And we have learned a few things since Itard's day. I'm encouraged by Genie's progress. Genie is a child of disturbed parents in—where else?—Los Angeles, who spent her entire childhood, from the time she was twenty months old until she was nearly fourteen, isolated in a small remote room, tied to a potty chair. Her mother made brief visits once a day to feed her. You can imagine the shape she was in four or five years ago when she was taken into custody. Now she has made enormous progress guided by experts and loving foster parents. She speaks and understands, reads and writes. Of course Genie was not a wild child; in some ways she was worse off than Victor. But here we have a child learning her native language after puberty. If her brain is that adaptive, John's may be, too."

Richard wanted to hear about Genie in detail. I related the story that my friend Victoria Fromkin, chairman of the Linguistics Department at UCLA had told when we gave our "double-header" talk on Victor and Genie. Genie's mother lived in fear of her husband, who often beat her. Although he wanted no children, after five years of marriage she became pregnant. He was furious and nearly strangled her. When their first child was born, the father had the baby kept in the garage so as not to hear her crying; at two and a half months, she died of overexposure.

The following year a second child was born. He had RH incompatible blood and died after two days. Three years later, another son was born, also RH incompatible. The mother did everything in her power to keep the child calm, unobtrusive and quiet. As he grew older he revealed increasing developmental problems (at three, for example, he was still not toilet-trained), so he was sent to live with his paternal grandmother for a while. There he made rapid progress and was returned home.

Three years later, Genie was born, with RH incompatible blood. When she was three months old, a physician found that she had a congenitally dislocated hip; he prescribed a Frejka pillow splint to keep her legs abducted. At her six-month checkup nothing seemed amiss, but at eleven months she was seventeen pounds underweight. The pediatrician removed the splint and recommended physiotherapy, but the father was opposed.

When she was almost two, Genie's life took a disastrous turn. Her paternal grandmother was killed by a car; her father, deeply embittered, moved his family into virtual seclusion in his dead mother's home. Genie was confined to a small bedroom, in which she was kept strapped to a potty chair, unclad. The father made the harness himself; to restrain her at bedtime, he sewed a sack in such a way as to hold her arms stationary—a kind of straitjacket. At night, if Genie was not forgotten in the chair, she was put into the restraining sack and then into a crib surrounded by wire mesh.

Genie remained in that room, hour after hour, day after day, week after week. She rarely heard a sound. There was no TV. The adjacent room had belonged to her grandmother; it was kept empty. Her mother was rapidly becoming blind and was totally subjugated by her father. She came to Genie's room only to feed her and stayed as briefly as possible. Increasingly the son took charge of his younger sister. If she made a noise, he beat her with a stick left in a corner of the room for that purpose. The father had taught Genie that when he barked she would receive a beating. Now he taught his son to do likewise, so he didn't have to enter the room to silence her. Months and then years went by.

When Genie was thirteen and a half, she and her mother escaped to her maternal grandmother. Shortly after, they went to apply for aid to the blind. When the social worker saw Genie and questioned the mother, she called the police. Genie's parents were charged with child abuse; on the day of the trial, her father committed suicide. Genie was admitted to the hospital at age thirteen and a half; she weighed fifty-nine pounds and was fifty-four inches tall. She was incontinent of urine and feces. She could not stand erect, run, hop, jump or climb. She was utterly mute. She salivated profusely and spat on everything; she rubbed the saliva in her hair. She reeked of saliva. She could not chew or swallow solid food (she had always been fed baby food). She did not react to hot or cold. She could not focus beyond ten feet, exactly the distance from her potty chair to the opposite wall, which for more than a decade was the outer limit of her visual field.

During the first six months in the hospital, Genie developed friendships with some of the staff. Slowly at first, she learned to recognize a few words; then in a great rush she began to learn the names of everything around her. By the time she was fourteen her life was coming together again. She had put on weight and learned coordination. She was more self-assured and self-aware. Most miraculously, she was learning her first language later than many scientists thought a child could. In a few weeks, she had brought down the most elaborately constructed theories, had refuted the so-called critical period for language acquisition, whether its upper reaches were placed at four years of age, as one school would have it, or at twelve, as another argued with equal vehemence. She had revealed all the specious argumentation for what it was. She had hundreds of words in her recognition vocabulary, as well as some spontaneous speech. Over the next six months, the complexity of the sentences she could comprehend and produce grew gradually. She started following stories. In January of 1972, when she was nearly fifteen, Genie used language for the first time to reflect about a past event. From then on, she spoke about her past, including her confinement. For example,, she said, "Father hit arm. Big wood. Genie cry." Soon she was using language to lie, and to manipulate others.

Genie made parallel progress in sensory, motor and social skills. She explored the world around her hungrily. But she spoke infrequently. Another problem that was especially recalcitrant was her public masturbation: chair backs and arms, doorknobs and car handles— all manner of things and places suited her. Nowadays, Genie is in a foster home. Susan Curtiss, a linguist who worked with her over the years, has written a book about her called *Genie: A Psycholinguistic Study of a Modern-day "Wild Child."* Genie's language is not normal. She has problems controlling her voice. When she speaks, her use of sounds is variable and unpredictable at times. Genie was taught some signs from the American Sign Language, and that seemed to help her speech and her communication; now her sentences often contain both speech and sign. She comprehends much of English grammar but not all. For example, she understands comparatives and negation, but not tenses. Her sentence production lags far behind her comprehension.

In Genie's dismal story we can find a ray of hope for John. In some ways, her experience was the more terrible of the two. She was restrained and he was not. She was cut off from social contact longer and began her rehabilitation later. Yet she made it, well, most of the way back into the fold. Perhaps John can, too.

This story led Richard to recall a boy named Peter he had seen many years before at a hospital in New England.

"There was a fire in an apartment building and the firemen found this thirteen-year-old terrified 'wild boy.' He was a mountain of flesh, four hundred and thirty pounds, and his hair was a tangled mass hanging to his waist. He had never seen anyone but his mother; he couldn't walk and hadn't been out of his bed for years. The firemen said he smelled so bad they couldn't stay in the room with him. Peter's mother was a severely retarded woman who worked (for the city of Boston!) and just left the boy alone every day. We cleaned him up and within a few weeks he was losing weight, walking and, like Genie, improving his physical skills very rapidly. He could speak and socially was like an eight- or nine-year-old—not normal but not nearly as badly off as Genie. Peter had one possession which I'm convinced saved him from total isolation: he had a TV set by his bed and he kept it on all day! He could hear people talk and see them interact. It's the old story which we keep rediscovering. Kids need to be touched, played with, talked to. Without that, development suffers in ways which we can only partly reverse. We should add something to our list of possible causes of John's abnormal development: isolation and neglect in some Burundi hut."

Flight 493 had taken us back across France, over the Alps, down the west coast of Italy. Now our captain pointed out the lights of Rome. Across the Mediterranean to Africa, invisible in the darkness. Over the Sahara, across the Tropic of Cancer, Mount Jabal Marrah, the Albert

Nile, the Sudan, Zaire, Lake Kivu, across the equator. At five-thirty the sun struck the horizon and lighted the ocean of clouds below. Shortly after seven we descended, breaking clear to see Lake Tanganyika surrounded by mountains, with Bujumbura at its head.

It's a small airport, dilapidated and forbidding, and we are wiped out from lack of sleep. David Kaeuper from the embassy is there to meet us. Ambassador David Mark and his wife Betty come over to shake hands, explain that it would be better if they didn't spend time with us before we clear customs, and disappear. Great consternation over our nine pieces of luggage. Two tape recorders? Five cameras? Over a hundred rolls of film?? The customs officer delicately unpacked everything and rolled his eyes toward heaven. We are in trouble!

A priest in a white cassock bustles up. He is Father Pagé—burly, enthusiastic, helpful. Pagé sails into the customs officer in French and Kirundi, with a great deal of name-dropping in both languages, and almost wins him over. He finally goes off to convince "my friend the head customs officer," and moments later gates open magically and we sweep through to a brigade of teenagers, who haul our luggage to the cars. I send telepathic thanks to Vince Ollivier for thinking to get us in touch with these fathers. The kids load us into Kaeuper's car. He tips them, confirming with Pagé that he gave the right amount; then he leaves and Pagé tips them all again.

The ride into town went quickly. Dense green vegetation, lush and wet, slipped past. Many tall blacks were working along the mud road. In the distance I could make out the purple mountains of the Rift, which divides the Nile and Congo basins. We got from Pagé the standard warning about talking politics: don't! We ease past a group of blacks cutting the roadside vegetation with razor-sharp machetes. I feel very nonpolitical. We stopped while some men finished raking a section of road. Nearby two young men were selling bananas next to a lean-to. My mind's eye framed them: as backdrop, the forested valley which sloped away from the road. Immediately behind them, a banana palm, its huge frontons casting an umbrella of shade over the boys. The lean-to, on closer inspection, was a kind of porch: the framework was of striplings; the roof of dried leaves; the side walls, reaching waist-high, were made of reddish stones embedded in the ubiquitous red clay. Everything had some cast of burnt sienna: the road of course, the shoulders, but also the car, the banana palms, the white stucco walls of the house from which the porch depended—everything was covered with a fine reddish-brown silt. It was in the very air; perhaps it was that which gave the warm, moist air a special scent—I can only describe it as not unpleasant. Take the top off a pot in which you are cooking beans and breathe deeply the warm, moist and musky odor; this scent was everywhere as the silt was everywhere. It covered the grimy barefoot boys, too. Their feet were sienna, their shorts beige and sienna, their shirts, blue and sienna, their faces, dark black. One stood at attention, the golden stalk poised shoulder-high in his left hand; the other clowned when he saw me gawking and, I think, entreated me in Kirundi to try a banana. The car lurched forward and the boys slipped behind.

At the embassy, Pagé left us, promising to arrange an interview tomorrow with the archbishop of Gitega—he'll call us. We settled down with hot coffee in Kaeuper's office and barraged him with questions. We are both witheringly tired; I have begun to have diarrhea without yet tasting the water (must be psychosomatic), but we are too excited to accept David's suggestion that we sleep first and talk later.

Kaeuper is about thirty; articulate and direct, he obviously wants to be helpful. He is informally dressed in tan slacks and an open shirt, and he wears a pinky ring. He started off by saying that he didn't know if the monkey story was true. "But everyone here believes it. The kid is a celebrity in Burundi. Hey, Carrie, come in a second. Ask my secretary, she's seen him."

Here was the first person we had talked to who had actually seen John, and the boy had obviously made a powerful impression.

"My husband and I were in Gitega. We just asked if we could see him and they promptly brought him out." What's he like? "He holds himself like a monkey, runs hunched over with his arms low. He has a terrific grip. My husband was amazed that a little kid could squeeze that hard. He likes bananas and people with beards." Have you heard the monkeys here? Does he really sound like them? "Yes, he does; he chirps and cries like a monkey." Do they let just anybody see him? "I guess so; of course we left a thousand francs as a contribution to the orphanage."

David believes that soldiers had brought John to missionaries, who in turn brought him to an orphanage somewhere; from there he was taken to the ward for the insane in Bujumbura. He feels we can get permission to go into the south and find the soldiers and missionaries —a letter from the archbishop will help. He offers a few words of orientation. The Batutsi, "the tall people," are aristocratic, aloof, protocol conscious. They had never really been subjugated by the Belgians and do not act like former colonials. Be ultra-polite and totally apolitical with the bureaucracy. As for the simple Burundi farmer, he will be polite, wary and obtuse. Burundians lack simple motor and organizational skills that Westerners take for granted: they have trouble hammering a nail; they can do routine tasks, but they forget what they have been taught if there is a day's break in their training; people who manage construction crews go crazy training them to level and square corners. David went on to mention a doctor, Frederico Bartoli, with the World Health Organization. "He knows everybody." Can he introduce us to that Russian psychiatrist who was identified in the newspaper as the one who cared for John in the psychiatric ward? "Zarotchintsev? Well, I'm not sure he is still in Burundi, but if he is . . ."

Richard and I left the embassy through a double set of steel-barred doors and walked into the brilliant morning sun. Across the road there's a coffee market, burlap bags filled with beans, men in red and gold robes haggling in Kirundi. I see a dilapidated garage doing no business and a nice-looking gift shop, its window filled with ashtrays and eggs of malachite, also doing no business.

The embassy guest apartment proved quite grand—three bedrooms, air conditioning, kitchen, terrace, dining and living rooms, and a house boy, Pio, who speaks some French. I asked Pio to stay on the alert for Father Pagé's call while Richard and I collapsed. Each time the phone rang, I made a dash across the apartment, but it was always some mysterious other thing resolved by Pio in Kirundi.

An hour's sleep took the edge off our exhaustion. Then we

changed money at the bank: a Burundi franc sells for roughly a penny (one dollar bought ninety francs). We decided to walk to the White Fathers' mission armed with David's map of Bujumbura (I had called them several times but couldn't get through). We found the mission, and as I thought, their phones were out of service. Pagé had left in his car and they didn't know when he would return. Let's eat!

Bujumbura has some Western buildings, but most of the people live in simple stucco barracks or shacks with corrugated tin roofs. It seemed more like a giant village than a city, and after Paris, it was hard not to find it decrepit and filthy. We lunched at Cristoff's Greek restaurant under a tropical bower complete with parrot. It was very hot and humid. The food looked vaguely Greek but was different from any I'd had in Greece or the United States. A huge bowl of vegetable soup was followed by hard pungent cheese fried in fat and garnished with a lime. Then a moussaka made with macaroni—a lion-sized chunk of it—and a tomato and scallion salad, which I resisted (per State Department instructions). Four courses *(service compris)* plus beer and coffee came to three dollars each. I felt a little guilty spending the equivalent of two days of Pio's wages.

From our veranda table I could see passers-by on the rue de Saio. I wondered whether the physical differences between Bahutu and Batutsi would be as obvious as their political rivalry. It wasn't, at least not to my eyes. There were many who seemed ill, some with obvious physical deformities that Richard said were the result of polio, and others, perhaps suffering from malaria, who just looked worn out.

By the end of the meal we had formed a rough plan: first, get back to the apartment to see if Pagé has arranged for us to see the bishop. It will be important to get his advice and help, as we'll most likely have to travel to remote and politically nervous areas of the country. Later, we should have time to visit the local hospital, interview psychiatrist Zarotchintsev and check out a medical laboratory, Forami, which Kaeuper had recommended. It will be important to know if they can do the blood and urine analyses we will need from John. Then tomorrow we head for Gitega. Kaeuper told us whom to see first: Septime Bizimana, the provincial governor whom we must consult if we are to work in his province.

Back to the apartment—no word from Pagé—and on to the embassy. Dr. Bartoli joined us—a dashing, charming, enthusiastic man of about fifty. He whisked us over to the hospital, on the way astonishing us by saying that John was in all probability a mongoloid and that it was known he had a brother who had died.

The Prince Regent Charles Clinic is in the Buyenzi section. Great crowds of people were waiting around. Bartoli wheels through them, with us in his wake. Many healthy-looking women in colorful flowing robes with babies mounted on their backs—this must be the maternity ward. Others terribly maimed—a soldier on a stretcher on the ground, bleeding. Shit on a staircase, crowded wards, stark, dingy; men stacking loaves of bread. At the psychiatrist's office Bartoli introduced us, explaining our mission. Dr. Zarotchintsev gave us a warm welcome. He seemed bemused and full of wonderment that we would come so far. An hour's intensive discussion ensued in which I formed the impression of a highly intelligent, humane and competent doctor—fluent in French, interested in us, our country, our ideas, our medical practices. The most outgoing Russian I had ever met. After a while we were joined by his *responsable de service* (equivalent to a head nurse) M. Laurent, a Burundian with the job, I gathered, of managing a psychiatric ward with two nurses and a hundred and twenty adult patients.

Zarotchintsev states that he found the boy John in the ward among these hundred-odd psychotic adults, when he arrived in Bujumbura in March 1974. The boy had already been there two years. (Laurent went off to check the dates: John was admitted June 13, 1972.) This contrasts with Barritt's account and destroys his theory that the boy may have wandered into the wilds when his parents were killed in the uprising in the spring of 1972.

Second surprise: Laurent says the boy was brought to the hospital from the Bujumbura orphanage where he had been taken by his father, who is still alive! On cross-examination, he doesn't *know* that—*"on m'a dit que . . ."* He promises to put us in touch with the orphanage so we can interview those who received and cared for the boy.

Third surprise (and fourth, fifth, etc.): Zarotchintsev mocks all the claims of monkey symptoms. The boy is a garden-variety imbecile with one peculiarity: he flails his hands against his forehead, a habit that has produced calluses on the forehead and on the backs of his hands. These epileptiform movements are accompanied by cries, and the seizures last about three minutes and subside. (Curiously, Itard reported that Victor had "spasmodic movements, often convulsions.") The cries are like those of any infant. He does not run on all fours. He is far from agile. He sleeps like any other child, not squatting.

To take care of John, Zarotchintsev had taken the reasonable step of finding him a surrogate mother, Thérèse, whom John had learned to recognize; when he was hungry, he would go up to her and let out cries. In fact that was about the only intelligent thing he did. Did he ever hide food as Victor had done? Never!

The medical workup had proven negative. Head X-rays, blood tests, stool examination (surprisingly) negative. Lumbar puncture negative. Neurological exam negative, except right tendon reflexes a little slower than left, or vice versa—he can't remember which. Impossible to do an EEG (electroencephalogram). The equipment has been broken for years. Could we go over the dossier? Dossiers are not maintained as such because there are too many patients, but there is a register where symptoms and treatments are recorded. Must ask Laurent for that. Zarotchintsev initiated requests to have the boy transferred to the Gitega orphanage (why Gitega and not Bujumbura?). This took about six months. In the interim, he gave John Largactyl (chlorpromazine) and Neuroleptyl (diazepam). Zarotchintsev said that in children—he estimates that John is now nine or ten—you have to give repeated small injections, which proved impractical. Of course John would not swallow pills. The treatment also included vitamins, and for some time they loosely bound John's hands together, to discourage head-flailing. Although John sometimes flailed with both hands, he usually did it with his right hand only, while emitting cries and rolling his eyes upward in their sockets. Zarotchintsev's diagnosis: John is an imbecile with Jacksonian epilepsy. (As described by Hughlings Jackson, this is a type of epilepsy in which abnormal movements begin in a certain part of the body—say, the left fingers—and progress until the whole body is involved in a grand mal seizure. The brain site controlling the part where the seizures originate is called the epileptic focus.)

Probable etiology of John's disease: infection during the first year of life, perhaps malaria leading to encephalitis or meningitis.

At this point, an odd-looking Russian doctor joined us without an introduction and sat in silence. I had encountered this routine before, in the Soviet Union; lest there be any question about their activities, scientists there prefer, or are required to have, a colleague present during meetings with foreigners. Bartoli bounced in to take us back to the embassy. "A case of mongolism, right?" "No," said Zarotchintsev, "probably encephalitis, and there is no history of a brother who died." "But there is a father," Laurent broke in. "Yes, I have heard that he has a father whose identity is known or can easily be found." On our way out, I proposed that we bring John back to the clinic to redo the studies, and Zarotchintsev generously agreed to give us all the help he could.

At the embassy, Bartoli called Governor Septime Bizimana in Gitega and asked him to see us and lend us all possible aid, then left a message at the Gitega hospital to say we would come by there, too. Just as we were leaving, Father Tuhabonye called from the orphanage. He was warm and cordial: John is waiting to see you; you must stay with us at the archdiocese; we have a report for you.

David came by to collect us for dinner at his house. How kind everyone has been! How shall we ever begin to reciprocate? Burundi may not be the ambitious young diplomat's first choice of assignments, but it has its perquisites: a large, elegant house in the hills overlooking Bujumbura and Lake Tanganyika. "It was built by a Belgian colonist," explained David, "and these two fellows are the Zamus—my night guards." Two blacks sat cross-legged on the porch, everything but their faces covered by robes. Other signs of security were the locked iron grilles on the downstairs doors and windows and a radiophone for quick communication with the embassy. We drank a Pimm's (nothing to recommend it, but they have to use their mangoes), listened to African music, admired our host's many masks and ivory statues, and chatted about life in Burundi over a fine meal and dry wine (shipped in from France). Harriet Isom was there—the deputy chief of mission; also David's girlfriend, Brenda Bowman, who is with the British Council (something like the Peace Corps), and Maggie Crocker, an English teacher. We told them what we had found out and I talked about my investigation of Victor.

Brenda had a sobering warning for us: what constitutes a good account of events is not the same in Burundi as it is in America. In this country in which most are eking out a subsistence, and in which news is carried from place to place by minstrels and individuals on business, the imperatives of survival and even, indeed, good rhetoric, may be more important than the truth. This caution agreed entirely with Ethel Albert's account of how culture controls speech in Burundi. She argued in the *American Anthropologist* that the Barundi perceive a steady diminution of power from God (Imana) to the King (mwami), to the princes (baganwa), to the nobles (abafasoni) to the herders (Batutsi) down to the Hutu peasants; that those at the bottom of the order see the arbitrary emotional exercise of personal power as the major force determining their lives; and that, therefore, the main role of language is to aid in the battle for survival by manipulating the actions of the more powerful through an appeal to their emotions. This rhetorical skill is called *ubgenge,* "successful cleverness." Albert illustrates this skill with a presumably true (*ubgenge*-free?) story.

A Murundi chief was very rude to a young Murundi agricultural officer. Instead of doing as he was told, collecting a labor force to start a coffee plantation, the chief went off to drink with one of his favorite tenants. When his delinquency was discovered, the chief was roundly scolded by the agricultural officer and assured that a report would be made to the higher authorities, the Belgian senior agricultural officer of the region. In due course, the summons came. The chief ordered his wife to fill three huge baskets with food, and he dressed in his finest robes. With his porters carrying the baskets, he proceeded to the office of the Belgian administrator. He was accused of refusing to provide workers to plant coffee, of rudeness as well as disobedience to the junior officer present, of permitting his cattle to graze on the plot designated for the coffee plantation.

On hearing the accusation, the chief looked very grieved and surprised. "Sir," he said, with all the respect and elegance his education enabled him to muster, "I have never seen this person. Since he knows my lands, perhaps he is the one about whom my tenants complained a few weeks back as demanding beer and getting drunk and disorderly." He waited a moment for his statement to take effect, counting on the suspicion of a national weakness for beer and a tendency to false report to be transferred from him to the junior officer. He then went on: "I am here because I have heard that you are suffering from famine. Here are the few humble baskets of food I could assemble in haste, but do not fear, there are many more on the way. I wish you all health."

Of course the administrator was furious with his junior officer and very favorably impressed by the chief. The officer was punished, and the chief was courteously released. On the way home the chief passed a church. Being a good Christian, he stopped to pray. He addressed himself to God, confessing his false accusation of the young agricultural officer, a fellow Murundi and a fellow Christian. He explained to the Lord that he knew he had sinned, but he begged forgiveness. "Oh, God, surely you will pardon me. Since you did not save me, I had to save myself."

The conversation turned to recreation in Bujumbura. What do you do for fun here? "Watch the hippos bathe in Lake Tanganyika. There are a yacht club and a riding club," said Brenda, "but the people who go there are so insensitive. Can you believe teenage children calling black adults 'boy'? Mostly we travel on our days off."

Harriet had just been to see the gorillas. There are only a few tribes of gorillas left, and one of these is in the hilly forests of neighboring Zaire. It's a hard trek in to photograph them. The gorillas are very gentle by nature and are protected, but often white hunters shoot them. One hunter who shot a female was tracked down and killed by the male, Harriet told us. The game warden recounted that some time ago he took home and bottle-fed a deserted infant he had found. When it was older, he returned it to the tribe and placed it near a receptive female. She took the baby but was not able to raise it and it died. The next time the warden came into the area, the gorillas came forward and held up the dead baby as if to show him what had happened to it.

We left the dinner at eleven with more than two hours of work still ahead of us. In the apartment Richard and I sat at opposite ends of the dining table recording the day's events—it was imperative not to sleep until we had written down all manner of facts and impressions and had planned for the following day.

V

FIRST
IMPRESSIONS

It is morning, and I can see the banana palms in the bright sunlight from my bed. Sleep and adventure are wrestling for control of my mind. I compromise and reflect on what we have learned so far. John was admitted to the hospital in June of 1972 and transferred to the orphanage only a year ago, so soldiers could not have captured him in the woods in 1974, as Barritt claimed, but only before 1972. And Barritt was wrong on another count: the boy could not have begun his career in the wild as a result of the Hutu massacre because that, too, was in the spring of 1972. Okay, then he was in the wild before 1972. Zarotchintsev says he's just an idiot, not a feral child, but Pinel said the same thing about Victor. Does Zarotchintsev have any independent evidence that John is brain-damaged? No. How does he explain John's monkey traits? He denies John runs on all fours or sleeps squatting. The calluses are from self-abuse. The fanning is epilepsy—but the description doesn't match epilepsy. And the monkeylike chattering? No explanation. It's time to have a look.

At the embassy, Kaeuper bargains with a driver who will take us the hundred-odd kilometers to Gitega. He introduces us to an Italian missionary, Father Masseroni, who is headed to the interior and will ride with us as far as Muramvya. He is dressed entirely in black, a short, chunky man with Sicilian features, a warm, shy smile and heavily accented, pedantic English. The taxi races through the outskirts of Bujumbura at breakneck speed, scattering the crowd in the road onto the shoulders. I glimpse stately women in brightly colored robes bearing children on their backs and balancing tall baskets on their heads; a bent old man with a staff; two boys carrying a large stalk of bananas; the stub of a man riding in a hand-propelled cart. African faces, sculpted in black ivory.

The road is curving and steep but newly paved, and we climb rapidly into the mountains, with vast panoramic views of the valley and Lake Tanganyika behind us. Although Burundi is one of the most densely populated countries in Africa, there are virtually no villages or towns. Thatched mud huts are scattered across the countryside, most hidden in groves of banana trees. The people till their small parcels of land nearby, making a patchwork of the hilly terrain. For centuries, land has been parceled out to the male members of the family; thus the patches of land have become smaller and smaller. There is less than an acre of arable land per capita in Burundi. We pass coffee and banana crops, and signs announce an experimental tea plantation; the government is trying to introduce new crops. Soon we have surmounted the great Congo-Nile Divide; the source of the Nile is found to the south along this range, on the eastern slope. The central and eastern plateaus, toward which we began our descent, are among the most densely populated regions of the country. Since there is little trouble with the tsetse fly in the uplands, cattle herders and farmers have put every square meter of land to use. Happily, our route will not lead us further east, where the terrain descends into hot, humid and disease-ridden plains and savannahs.

THE WILD BOY OF BURUNDI

Father Masseroni has overcome his initial reticence and regales us with anecdotes, whether from Christian desire to help orient us or from the sheer love of storytelling, I can't say. Much later, we realized it was neither; he was introducing us to a central fact of life in Burundi society, one that had become a part of him from living there: the transmission of culture, law, religion and news by word of mouth, by storytelling. Whatever were the imperatives of this performance, factual accuracy and conciseness were not foremost; it was art as well as science, as we would find to our dismay as we tried to piece together John's story. Take, for example, the father's stories about death: our recorder caught most of them intact.

A woman came to the mission to say that her husband was dead and she wanted to marry again. Was it true? Her hearing was held and witnesses came. Strangely enough, her husband was among those who came to testify—the husband that she had said was dead. This was our second reminder that factual accuracy depends on the demands of the situation. "If anyone says of a man," Ethel Albert wrote of Burundi culture, "that he has no children and there will be nobody to bury him, this must not be taken literally, especially if it is said in the presence of the man's sons. It means that some of his sons have died." Similarly, to say that "I went to Paul's house but there was no beer" means that a few quarts were downed but that the supply was insufficient or the reception was unfriendly. Stylized exaggeration is common throughout the culture, especially in bartering; a generous person may be called *mwami* or even *imana*. Father Masseroni went on to tell us other stories about death with a different moral—namely, that rampant poverty and disease end by devaluing all life, including healthy lives. In one region of Burundi a religious sect that encouraged its followers toward cannibalism was becoming widespread. To placate or comply with the divinity, followers had to burn a human victim and consume it. Some people disappeared like this without leaving any trace. Some time ago a pregnant woman was killed. Her body was found horribly mutilated and eaten. Once a young girl found herself in an area that was some distance from her house. She was out trying to gather beans for planting. She saw that night was coming and she found herself even further from her hut, so she asked for hospitality from a family in the area. Here it is very frequent that people have to sleep outside or away from home; normally people feel themselves honored to offer hospitality to travelers or to people out away from their huts. It is this way also in the missions. Every mission offers free hospitality, and offers it with great joy. This girl, then, set herself in the small corner of the hut in which she was staying, and she put down her sack of beans. When it was time for sleep, she went to lay herself down with the two children of the father of the house. The father of the household, however, came over and told her to put herself in the first sleeping place, the one closest to the door. The girl intuited that something was going on. And when it was dark and silent, slowly she moved herself between the two sisters. At about midnight the father came in. He wanted to appropriate that bag of beans. He lightly touched with one hand the first person in the sleeping bunk, as if to assure himself of the person's presence. Then he delivered a sharp hatchet blow, killing the person. He was convinced that he had murdered the guest, and the body was immediately buried in the dark and mysterious night. When everything returned to calmness, the young girl quietly and furtively escaped from the hut, and quickly made her way away from there. She went to the commissioner and reported what happened and immediately the gendarmes left with her. By dawn they had reached that hut, led by this courageous girl. The gendarmes knocked on the door. The father answered.

"Have you offered hospitality to a girl this last night?" they asked.

"No, no one has been here knocking on our door," the man replied.

"Well, here is the girl who stayed here last night," the gendarmes said, indicating the girl who had come with them. Could you imagine his shock and dismay? It was only then that the evil father realized that he had killed his own daughter.

Father Masseroni paused as we traversed a high plateau, past a bustling open-air market taking place in a vast clearing. It is a happening East African style; there are countless foci of activity scattered about on the red clay. Here a woman in a brightly colored red-and-blue dress is bending over a woven basket sorting greens; two or three other women are seated on the ground nearby with their own baskets full of vegetables. There a man in a white robe stands next to a case of bottles —perhaps the beer merchant. A little further, a boy in a plaid shirt is emptying a large jug of milk into a pan on the ground. Then there are clotheslines strung from sticks, bearing swatches of cloth, brilliant colors in the dazzling sunlight: royal blue, crimson, brightest aquamarine. A knot of young men stand in a circle talking. To their left is an opening in the crowd where garments are spread out on a ground cloth. And scattered between all these foci, and moving among them, hundreds of people in almost as many postures: some are ambling singly or in pairs; some, bearing great baskets on their heads, move in dignified, erect and measured gait; some take a moment's respite from their burden, one arm gripping the clay pot or the basket or the bundle of faggots on their head, forming a sideways V silhouetted against the sky; some teeter on bicycles, moving ahead unsteadily as they converse; some are bending over forward, and some, stretching their backs, are bending over backward; and some are lying on the ground, apparently asleep.

The sight of a coffee plantation reminds Father Masseroni of his past efforts to cultivate coffee near his mission, in the village of Mivo. The cultivation of coffee is the most profitable thing in Burundi, he said. The state promotes and encourages it. One of the renowned brands of coffee is that of Mivo. In order to favor the coffee plantations, the state gives away plants and forbids substituting other cultivating where there is cultivation of coffee. A few months ago the mission foreman, Don Minghetti, made a request to the community of Ngozi for a hundred and fifty coffee plants. Around the mission there is land that will be cultivated for coffee. The request was granted, and on the day of distribution a trustworthy man went early in the morning to pick up the promised coffee plants. But at Ngozi, right near the city hall, there was a brawl: the crowd pressed against the gates of the warehouse, which gave way, and some natives, the most astute and the quickest, illegally took possession of all the coffee plants. There was general indignation all around.

Among one of the astute who managed to get some of the coffee

FIRST IMPRESSIONS

plants was someone from Mivo. A few days after the incident he let
it be known that he was willing to sell coffee plants for a franc apiece.
Don Minghetti confronted him with this dishonesty and threatened to
denounce him. In this way he succeeded in gaining back seventy of the
coffee plants, and they were then planted on the land that had been
prepared for them. Occasionally, in the evening, while Father Masseroni recited the rosary, he visited the little plantation, to check on
the progress of the plants. But one evening last week when he'd gone
out, he'd had a terribly bitter surprise. The coffee plants had been
stolen. Only seven were left. One does as much as one can to help these
people, and then in the end one finds oneself having to submit to such
searing deceptions. There's a proverb in Burundi that goes: "The evil
of one falls on all of the family." The foreman of the mission has
decided on a drastic response. For two weeks there will be no medicine
distributed. And recently there has been an invasion of sickness and of
false sickness. Mivo is possibly the only mission in which medicine has
been given out freely to all.

Father Masseroni's stories made the miles slip by; the last one we
heard was his tale of the "penetrating fleas." Every night Abbé Simon
used to call Peter and Tony so that they could take out the fastidious
fleas. Don Minghetti instead used to call Simone or Andrea. The
operation was always hard, long, tiring and painful. The flea is black
and very tiny. It prefers to penetrate and nest underneath the foot. In
that spot under the foot you notice it almost immediately because it
creates an insistent itching that at night doesn't let you sleep. The black
is especially good at removing them. Large or small, he is always armed
with a large pin, and it is his particular talent to extract these fleas.
Often you see children and adults sitting along the road or along the
land with their foot in their hand, intent on extracting these deadly
fleas. If the flea manages to get under the skin, it devours blood and
can bring infection. Almost all the children at the mission are already
missing their toenails, for the fleas have eaten them. The rain partly
destroys these little animals, but during the dry season the fleas can
torture human feet at will.

The last night of the year we had a long conversation after dinner about the penetrating fleas, and I was bragging about being allergic to them. I had been in Africa for more than seventy days, and up to that point I had not yet met them. I was almost a little sad. When I went to bed I carefully searched my feet and I discovered a small black dot surrounded by a yellowish halo; in fact, it was a penetrating flea. I had been carrying it for a few days without even noticing it. I got a needle and I performed the delicate operation, and in a few days my foot was healed. I was content; finally, I had met the penetrating flea. Up until now it has been the only one, but I can assure you that every evening I check my feet by candlelight. I don't really feel like finding one day that one of my feet has been eaten by one of these penetrating fleas.

Yesterday morning there was the changing of the guard in the kitchen. Tony and Andrea switched jobs with Peter and Simone. In their turn, our boys enjoy and profit from their day off, which they dedicate to working in their fields or for their families. I found myself in the morning at the work site. At about eleven-thirty I saw all the children come out of the school for their required half-hour of gym. The students reached the sports field and remained there, tranquilly waiting for their teacher, who was somewhat delayed because she was talking to a colleague. Three children immediately began to profit from this waiting time to try to extract fleas from three of their friends. The teacher arrived and immediately discovered this breach of discipline. The six children were subject to rather strict punishment. The three patients received forty whacks on their bare feet, and the three sur-geons received twenty. With my heart full of pity I watched the children grit their teeth with pain. Not one tear lined their faces. They have truly a great capacity for suffering. I would have liked to intervene, but not knowing the scholastic rules of Burundi, I was worried about some kind of complication. This horrifying episode told me that we are really very far from true civilization, that civilization which above all respects human beings in all of their dignity, in all of their rights. Respect for whatever kind of human beings, whether we are talking about Tutsi or Hutu children.

We pass through a grove of tall trees where the air is laden with the scent of eucalyptus. Father Masseroni says a few words in Rundi to the driver, who pulls over at a fork in the road. The little priest slips out of the car and turns to wave goodbye. He wishes us good luck in our mission.

At noon we arrive in Gitega, in front of the old German fort that now houses the offices of the provincial governor. At the turn of the century, the Germans had moved the seat of government from Bujumbura to Gitega in order to have more control over the mwami, the Tutsi monarch, and the ganwa, the princes of royal blood who headed the four dynastic clans; Gitega had long been the ancient seat of these rulers.

A young man dressed in the white tunic and slacks of a civil servant came forward to greet us. I remember it well because it was the first of many similar receptions we would receive as we traipsed about the countryside: his right hand was extended while his left grasped his forearm lightly; we looked at each other openly, even warmly, as we shook hands, and I read candor in his face, a willingness to share our concerns but not deference, and restrained curiosity. We were indeed a curious group gathered in the bright midday sun in front of the dazzling white fort. Two Americans, a great rarity outside of the capital, in suit and tie (even more rare, and rightly so), a taxi laden with supplies. He gave the driver instructions to the archdiocese; we would see the governor later.

We passed through the town square in a cloud of red dust, but I could make out a few weather-beaten storefronts labeled in French —a tobacconist, a pharmacy, a dry-goods store. We rattled over a washboard road past a parish and a military prison and drove up the broad gravel avenue of the archdiocese. The vicar, Father Juvenal Kadogo, greeted us in front of a large and handsome beige-brick church that was being demolished. The bricks are made by hand from the local clay, he explained, pointing to the reddish soil at our feet. But after forty years they have begun to crumble, and the church was starting to collapse. It is being reconstructed. The church looked as if a mammoth bulldozer had sheared off the chancel. Elsewhere the façade and sloping tile roof were covered by scaffolding made of stripped saplings. There were several enormous mounds of

THE WILD BOY OF BURUNDI

brick and debris, higher than a man and twice as wide.

The campus of the archdiocese includes some twenty buildings. Several provide classrooms and dormitories for teacher training. Students graduating from high school, he told us, are required to spend some time in the countryside as teachers. In this way the government hopes to stem the flow of educated youth from the farm to the city. The teachers come to the archdiocese for a few weeks of liberal arts study and then return to their villages. The other buildings include a convent, a refectory, and administrative offices. We leave off our things in our rooms, which are as plain as monks' cells—bare floor, table, chair, washbasin, cot—and follow the vicar to lunch.

There are eight of us at the table, including Archbishop André Makarakiza, a tall and singularly dignified man in his fifties, completely dressed in black, with a ready smile and an open face that bespoke, I felt, a spirit utterly without pretension. I told the story of our journey so far and asked for their observations and opinions of John. The archbishop had not seen him, but the vicar had, several times. John looks abnormal, but his coordination is good; he is very healthy and strong. He is a friendly boy who runs up to adults and tries to climb on them. He likes to slam doors. The vicar confirmed that John had been brought here directly from the hospital; he credited this not to Zarotchintsev but to the directress of the orphanage, Sister Nestor, who had heard about the boy and had gone to Bujumbura to arrange his transfer. The orphanage here, run by the church and staffed by volunteers, orphans themselves who live and work with the children, is better than the orphanage in the capital, run by the government and staffed by civil servants. And the climate in Gitega, some three thousand feet above sea level and hence free of malaria, is better for the children.

We leave the archdiocese and drive down a winding rutted track to the orphanage, which is perched on a hillside with a commanding view. In the near distance are the tops of evergreen and banana trees that have found a foothold partway down the slope. The view beyond is of boundless space save for the purple profile of some mountains in the farthest plane. The building overlooking the valley is L-shaped; its overhanging roof is red tile; its walls are covered in white stucco and are interrupted every few feet by tall windows. From the base of the windows, waist-high, to the concrete walkway the materials of construction are visible: beige stones forming a random mosaic in the reddish cement. The walkway runs the length of the L, and all the doors and windows open on to it. We look into the nursery, a small room dimly lit by the sunlight filtering in under the roof. It is crowded with some three dozen tiny metal cribs covered with netting, all empty at this hour. The next window is on a playroom, utterly bare except for a mat on the concrete floor and a large red ball. We pass another window and then a wooden "dutch" door that opens into a classroom with tables, chairs, and a blackboard. Next comes a sitting room for the staff and visitors: it, too, is bare except for the back seat of a station wagon, its springs protruding from the bottom, its stuffing protruding from the top. "Look!" Richard whispers. And there in the corner is John.

He is sitting cross-legged on the floor, eating with his fingers from a plate of food in front of him. Certainly he is a strange-looking child. From where I stand, nearly in front of him, I cannot see his pupils, only the whites of his eyes; his gaze is fixed rigidly off to the extreme right. His forehead is covered with scabs and calluses. His lips are pulled back over his teeth in an expression of pain or fear. His right hand flaps relentlessly up and down in front of his face, fingers splayed. He chatters constantly, his lips and cheeks vibrating to make bizarre—yes, monkeylike—sounds; he occasionally breaks into a screech while his body rocks back and forth.

Sister Nestor Nzisabira, an attractive, efficient-looking woman in a colorful robe and kerchief, brings in some chairs. She smiles when I try to get her name clearly. "Call me Sister Nestor; it's a man's name just as in your country." I try to block a thousand thoughts from my mind. So this is the boy we have come so far to see. Irrelevant. Dr. Livingstone, I presume. Silly. He's grotesque. You're unnerved. Look at the fanning, where did he learn it? That's not epilepsy; I bet Richard agrees. Come on, begin at the beginning.

"Sister Nestor, when did you first meet John?"

"I went to see him a year ago in the insane ward at the hospital."

I translate the question and answer for Richard, who is taking notes, but he signals he understands.

"What was he like then?"

"Much as he is now. He fanned his face, made noises, wouldn't eat solid food, wouldn't go to the toilet."

"How has he changed?"

"At first he wouldn't eat from a plate; he would turn it over on the ground and eat from the ground. But now he eats from a plate. And in the beginning, when he wanted to urinate, he would open his mouth and hold his penis and then urinate and defecate on the floor. Now, he takes off his pants, and when Petronille, who watches over him, sees that, she takes him to the toilet. But sometimes he forgets."

"What's the most intelligent thing he has learned?"

"When he is hungry he goes to the cupboard, takes his personal plate, and brings it to the cook. If it happens not to be mealtime, he will cry, screech, bang his head, throw a temper tantrum until we relent and feed him. Also, he opens and closes doors."

"How?"

"He holds down on the latch and pulls. But to close it he just slams it."

"Which hand does he use?"

"In the beginning he used both hands, but we taught him to use his right hand."

At this point, Petronille Sinibarura joined us: a very attractive teenager, an orphan herself she told us later. She was obviously impressed that we would travel halfway around the world to see her Johanni. Smiling impishly, she extended her right hand held with her left.

"What does Johanni like to eat?"

"Bananas. He bites off the top and scoops the meat out with his fingers."

"Anything else?"

"Rice. La pâte [pasta]. But nothing solid. He won't chew."

"What else does Johanni like to do besides eat?"

"Nothing much. He doesn't like toys or games. He stands alone in the corner by himself a lot. He won't play with the other children."

FIRST IMPRESSIONS

"Does he fight with them?"

"He ignores them."

But he doesn't ignore adults. John came up to me and climbed into my lap, facing me. I tried to engage his gaze, but try as I might he looked away. He moved restlessly, constantly twisting and turning, all the while chattering and fanning his face.

"Sometimes he's so restless at night, rocking in the crib, banging his hands or his head against the bars that we have to tie him down," Petronille said.

"Does he sleep squatting?" I asked.

"No, on his side."

"Have you ever seen him run on all fours?"

"No, but he walks with a lope." Petronille demonstrates a sort of prancing, skipping step, landing on her toes.

"Have you ever seen him climb?"

"Once I took him into a field and I hid behind a tree to see what he would do. He didn't climb a tree or run off; he just wandered around a little and began to cry."

"He cries like other children?"

"Yes, his eyes get red and tears run out. He laughs, too. Especially if you tickle him," Petronille replied. She takes John and demonstrates. For a moment he is like any child, squeaking with delight and rolling about in her lap.

"But he hates to have his head touched," she explains, placing her palm on top of his close-shaven head. John reaches up and dexterously removes her hand.

"Most of all he hates to have his eyes covered." And Petronille placed her hands over his eyes. Suddenly John screams for dear life, tears away from her and charges out of the room, with the four of us in hot pursuit. He runs the length of the porch, leaps into a garden where masons are working on a wall, and slams the gate in our faces. Then he strains to lift a large cinder block as if he might pick it up and throw it at us. Petronille is dissolved in mirth and we are silently impressed by the boy's unusual agility as we make our way back to the room.

"Is John a healthy boy?"

THE WILD BOY OF BURUNDI

"Yes, but he's deaf. Or, anyway, hard of hearing."

"How do you know?"

"Well, he doesn't speak, and often I call to him and he doesn't answer."

"Has he been sick?"

"He had diarrhea once for a few days. And a cold."

"Nothing else? Typhus? Malaria?"

"No."

"Can you think of anything else you'd like to tell us about him?"

"Sometimes he would get very excited and hit his head with his hands. Then we would tie them. Now if that happens, he'll come over and hold out his hands for them to be tied. He has an odd smell. He sweats more than the other children."

"How old do you think he is?" At three and a half feet tall, he appears five or six to us.

"Eight or nine. Maybe ten or more."

"Do you think he was raised by monkeys?"

"C'est ce qu'on dit. They say soldiers found him with monkeys and brought him to Bujumbura. He acts like a monkey."

Before long the children would be fed and put to bed, so it was agreed that we would return the next day to begin our study of John. Back in our rooms, I was relieved to change out of my suit. Then word arrived that the governor would see us at once. Off with the jeans, on with the suit. The governor, too, was dressed in a suit, threadbare and poorly fitting, when we met him in his home a few minutes later. He appeared in his late sixties or early seventies, a thin wizened old man with a toothless smile and a penetrating gaze. I would describe him as shrewd, but perhaps David Kaeuper had prejudiced me when he said that the governor is a cunning politician, the only civilian to survive in power when President Micombero replaced all the others with generals. He knew absolutely everything that was taking place in his province, and woe betide the man who didn't secure his authorization.

The governor's living room was spacious, with high ceilings, and there were nicely planted grounds that we could see from the windows. Yet the furnishings were plain and functional. There was no rug on the concrete floor, and the whitewashed walls made the room seem barren and spare. The governor noted our names carefully and introduced himself: Septime Bizimana. Before we began, his wife served us large glasses of delicious and refreshing beer. Beer made from bananas or sorghum is indispensable. Every ritual, contract, discussion and visit requires it, Father Kadogo later explained. I described at length the purpose of our mission. There had not been a well-documented case of a feral child since Victor of Aveyron in the last century. We must learn everything we can about John, not only for the sake of science but for his own sake if there is any possibility that we can help him. I hastened to add that the archbishop welcomed our investigation and had generously agreed to lodge us at the archdiocese.

I described the interviews we had conducted so far, and explained that since there was no record of the tests conducted on John at the hospital, we would want to bring him back there for additional tests. The governor was concerned about uprooting the boy. We saw no alternative, and I had the guarded hope that I could repair the machine for recording brain waves. If not, we would certainly try to have the missing parts shipped in.

It was Gitega, not Bujumbura, that really should receive help and spare parts, he protested. It was in the center of the country, well-situated, surrounded by three important reserves of nickel, the city of the future in Burundi. We readily saw his logic; whatever gifts are made should come to Gitega. What are their most urgent medical needs? Conceivably we could find a way to help. For example, why not approach the American embassy for medical aid? When nations try to help each other through their governments, he explained, rarely are the real needs met, and then only after long delays. Officials working at the paper level are too removed and uninformed. These problems must be solved at the human level, by people reaching out to one another. Dr. Barakamfitiye, head of the local clinic, could tell us about their needs.

"If John is truly a wild boy," he went on, "then science could repeat with modern technology the studies that had been done on Victor of Aveyron. Gitega is becoming a center of tourism because of the boy. I hope your report will be definitive, and it will not be necessary to study the boy further." How fully he seemed to understand my own frame of mind, our desire to get to the bottom of the mystery. Was he also saying that too many curious visitors were not welcome, or to the contrary, that once the boy's bona fides were known, tourists might come and spend some money here? Perhaps he is just defending the interests of the boy; John must not remain an object of study indefinitely.

In the end, the governor assured us of every possible assistance—even permission to travel in the Bururi region, which I had requested so we could seek out the soldiers who had captured John and brought him to the capital.

After dinner, we sat with eight priests in the refectory, including Father Pierre Tuhabonye, an important source for Barritt's article and the priest who had given John his name—after John the Baptist, he explained, who had also spent time in the wilderness. Father Tuhabonye is a handsome, trim man in his thirties with a lively intelligent look and ready wit. Like everyone we have met, he is thoroughly kind and considerate and is ready to do all he can to assist us. Pierre is the only priest in the group who speaks some English; they all speak French as well as their native Rundi. Father Melchior volunteered that a friend of his, a military chaplain, reported that John had been found by soldiers in the Bururi region, which is in the south (but not as far as Nyanza Lac, where Barritt had placed his capture). Could a child live wild in that area? On our trip to Gitega, we found the land so extensively cultivated that it would be impossible for a child to survive unnoticed in the countryside. Yes, but the Bururi region is more sparsely populated, he explained, and has a more rugged terrain. A child could easily roam there for months. We could find the chaplain, he replied to my question, by checking with military headquarters in Bujumbura.

Valéry Giscard d'Estaing's visit to Washington in the Concorde, announced on Burundi radio, prompted one priest to ask why the United States had not built a commercial supersonic plane. They seemed skeptical when I told them that concern about cost and pollution blocked the way. During this explanation I tried to keep my aplomb while some enormous tropical insect made strafing runs over my head. "That," said one of the priests with a rueful smile, "is the African Concorde."

The conversation turned to health in Burundi and then to the symptoms of our dinner companions. We agreed to examine a monk who had lost hearing in one ear, and a melancholy young instructor, not a clergyman, who was feeling fatigued. Back in our room, Richard cleaned the monk's ear canal and showed me my first view of the middle ear of a living patient. I was wide-eyed at the sight of the gaping hole where I expected to find an eardrum. Some years ago our visitor had developed a terrible earache followed by a drainage of pus. Undoubtedly he had had an infection of the middle ear and the accumulating pus burst the eardrum beyond repair. This situation was almost entirely preventable even before antibiotics, Richard said. A fine incision in the eardrum—a myringotomy—allows drainage; after the infection subsides, the slit heals. With antibiotics, the treatment is even simpler. We found that the monk had good perception of bone-conducted sound, showing that his auditory nerve was undamaged. Possibly an eardrum graft could restore hearing if the archdiocese would send him out of the country to have it done. I promised to urge this on the archbishop.

The young instructor had diabetes, and this, we explained, is the likely cause of his exhaustion, if he has not been taking enough insulin. We tested his urine with our sugar-sensitive dipsticks and found that he was spilling a great deal of sugar into his urine. He had been given insulin, but without a way to test his urine he was afraid to take very much. We promised to leave him our supply of dipsticks and told him that closer regulation of his insulin would help him to feel better.

When our visitors left, Richard and I reviewed what we had learned that day.

"The big question, Richard, is whether or not this boy has a hereditary defect."

"That's the first hypothesis. The second is still that he's a feral child."

"And the third is both. So far, we're exactly where Itard and Pinel were with Victor."

"Okay, and the fourth possibility is that he acquired brain damage later in life from malaria, typhus, measles, a tumor—you pick it. Take the first hypothesis. Suppose he's a garden-variety idiot, as Zarotchintsev calls him. Suppose it's hereditary. What's he got? There are hundreds of possibilities. Let's start with the metabolic disorders. Most of them show up in the blood or urine, but we won't know about that until we can run the tests back in the States. And they're all pretty rare."

"Let's see if we can rule them out from what we've seen so far."

"Phenylketonuria is the best known. Maybe one kid in twenty thousand is born missing a critical liver enzyme that converts an amino acid, phenylalanine, to another amino acid, tyrosine. The phenylalanine is converted instead to phenylketones, which are poison to developing brain cells. Severe mental retardation, restless hyperactive behavior, repetitive movements are the result. *Voilà* John. And I remember something Petronille said that may be important. She mentioned that John smells funny. PKU kids are often described as having a musty or animal-like odor. So let's put PKU on the list."

"I didn't notice an odor. Those phenylketones show up in the urine—phenyl ketone uria. That's what the dipsticks are all about?"

"Right," Richard answered. "You can prevent the effects of PKU with the proper diet, one that lacks the phenylalanine the liver can't metabolize. But you have to start the diet within a few weeks of birth. There are a couple of points against PKU here. One is that affected kids usually have blond hair and blue eyes like Paula, the girl we saw at Fernald. This is because phenylalanine is a precursor of the skin pigment melanin. Black kids very rarely have PKU."

"We'll know tomorrow when we use the dipsticks."

"Apart from PKU, there must be several dozen other disorders of protein metabolism. Most of them involve more physical signs than we are seeing—ataxia, for example. You've seen the staggering gait of an alcoholic. That's not our John. He has a sort of prancing toe gait."

"Okay, under metabolic disorders, we go with PKU."

"There's more. Disorders of sugar metabolism or lipid metabolism. Generally they go with an enlarged liver or spleen or both. You can feel that when you knead his belly. In some cases, there are changes in the appearance of the retina. We'll probably rule these out after the physical exam. Then there's Hurler's syndrome—gargoylism—but that ugly, he's not."

"Beautiful he's not either," I countered. "What does it take to qualify?"

"Short stature, clawlike hands and feet, crouching posture, wall-eyes, hearing loss, nasal discharge."

"Hold it, that's a pretty good score. I'll put it on the list."

"Come on, you've been to Notre Dame. John is no gargoyle. Anyway, we'll know from the physical: the liver and spleen should be enlarged. And we agree he's not a cretin. He's not even a funny-looking kid!"

"Medical jargon?" I asked.

"An FLK is what pediatricians call someone who isn't really bizarre-looking, just a bit odd. That 'funny' look often goes with retardation."

"It's hard to say with all the calluses and his peculiar expression. What about hydrocephalics, macrocephalics and microcephalics?"

"The cranial anomalies. Peter Rosenberger reminded us how important it is to get an accurate head measurement, and when we do, I can check it against a table of normal head circumference for a given height and age. But there's nothing peculiar about the shape of his head. The physical and X-rays will rule these out as well, I expect. Also, he's not mongoloid, as Bartoli thought. There are other anomalies of development: Laurence-Moon-Biedl syndrome, for example: mental retardation, stunted growth, pigmented retina, bizarre behavior, obesity and polydactylism. He's got a distended belly, but he's not obese and he doesn't have extra fingers. Talk about rare—few people have ever seen a case."

"I'll put it on the list, anyway. Are we through?"

"A history would help us a lot. Is he getting worse? Better? If his condition is stable, it probably rules out conditions like a brain tumor. Nutritional diseases don't seem right either. He would have to have a lot else wrong. He seems to have a focal condition involving language loss and repetitive movements, but physically he is very much intact."

"How about autism, Richard?"

"Disturbances of perception, delayed language, movement disorders, and of course, disturbed social relationships. Hmmm . . ."

"It seems to fit. He's got apparent hearing loss, avoids eye contact, no language and at least two movement disorders: the fanning and the toe gait. And he doesn't relate to the other kids."

"There is no specific test for autism. One way we can get a handle on it, and most of the other congenital disorders in the process, is to find out what John was like when he was an infant—say, from birth to age two or three. Autistic children definitely have symptoms by age two and a half to three."

"And we could also rule out prenatal infections and injuries."

"Most likely," Richard agreed. "For example, his mother could have had rubella—German measles—and transmitted it to the fetus. That can often can often lead to permanent brain damage and mental retardation. Same thing for syphilis. But I think we can rule out prenatal infections once we do the physical and the X-rays. Maternal rubella leaves heart defects, enlarged liver, abnormal bone growth. Syphilis leaves skin and bone lesions."

"What it amounts to is this. If the tests turn up something new —something wrong with his liver or his retina, for example—we may be able to confirm the first hypothesis: a defect present at birth. But if we don't learn more than we've seen so far, we can't rule it out until we trace his history."

"Yes, and we'll need his history if we're going to rule out a childhood disease, the fourth hypothesis. Maybe he caught malaria, for example, and that produced brain damage. Or measles or smallpox. In all those cases, the virus doesn't actually get into the nervous system. Instead, there's an immune reaction to the disease that causes brain swelling, damage to the nerves, and as a result, mental retardation and motor and sensory disorders. Some bacteria and viruses do attack the nervous system directly, of course, and he could have caught one of those—meningitis, for example. We can tap some cerebrospinal fluid and have it analyzed in the States to see what viral antibodies are present. But that won't tell us much, since he's probably had a low-grade case of everything at one time or another. A valuable test here will probably be the electroencephalogram; if there's diffuse brain damage it should show up. But autistic kids sometimes yield abnormal tracings and for all we know, prolonged social isolation might yield them, too."

"So if we find evidence of metabolic disorders or the like, we can adopt the first hypothesis; if we don't, we hold onto autism and childhood diseases, and trace his history. Remember, too, that there are childhood diseases that are not caused by infection. There's schizophrenia, developmental aphasia, epilepsy and maternal deprivation—perhaps he's spent too much time in orphanages and hospitals. In the process of tracing his life history, we can also follow up the feral angle: talk to the soldiers who caught him, try to find his parents. Don't forget the third hypothesis: he may have had a defect at birth *and* have been left in the wild—perhaps for that very reason."

"Maybe we'll know all tomorrow morning."

"Sleep tight. Remember where you are and don't forget your prayers."

"I'm going to pray for Laurence-Moon-Biedl syndrome: imagine being the ones to find a case!"

THURSDAY, MAY 27—GITEGA

Our day of examining John began with his urinating all over Richard. I had set up my tripod and camera on the patio, facing Richard, who was holding John in his lap. When the yellow stream began, we both dived for the dipsticks and pressed them on Richard's pants and in the pool forming on the concrete floor. The other orphans and staff looked on in wonder. The test for phenylketonuria was negative: John the Jungle Boy was not simply a PKU baby.

The rest of the morning was spent filming and tape-recording John. We examined him carefully and probed his vision, hearing, touch and coordination to see what other signs we could find of disease or feral rearing. Here is our workup.

THE WILD BOY OF BURUNDI

John is an unidentified Negroid boy appearing well developed and well nourished. His skin is dark brown, smooth and healthy, no major scars. There are rugosities on the ears, forehead and wrists—areas where he is seen to strike himself repeatedly. Palms normally creased. Head circumference, 51 cm., is that of an American eight-year-old; height, 196 cm., is that of an American five-year-old. Chest, 60.5 cm., crown-rump 46.5 cm., arm span 106 cm., and belly 60.5 cm. There are no facial abnormalities, the ears are not low or deformed. Teeth and gums are healthy. He has lost all of his deciduous teeth and has at least 24 permanent teeth; it's hard to see whether the 12-year molars are erupted yet. He gives no evident response to sound; however, a startle response was elicited by shaking a can of jacks behind his head. He apparently responds to bone-conducted sound, since he withdraws his head when a vibrating tuning fork is touched to his head but not when a stationary fork is applied. The pupils react briskly to bright light. Conjugate eye movements in all directions were observed. The gaze is generally averted, and he will actively avoid eye contact. He occasionally fixates on objects briefly—for example, to grasp some food—but more often the eyes are maximally averted either to the left or to the right. In that position, normal slight nystagmoid movements are noted. There is evidence of peripheral vision and visual recognition of food items. Hand-eye coordination is swift and accurate. There is optokinetic nystagmus, but we have been unable to elicit vestibular nystagmus.

The belly is distended, 60.5 cm. in circumference, but soft and nontender. Liver and spleen are not palpable. Brief auscultation of the chest revealed no abnormal breathing or heart sounds. John responds to pinpricks with withdrawal and crying. He has a good grip, can grasp slim objects between finger and thumb, but will occasionally let objects fall from his hand. He walks normally, runs rapidly but with a slight abnormality of gait—an exaggerated toe gait somewhat like prancing. He laughs when tickled, but we have seen no social smiling. Sometimes he lays his lips back over his teeth rather like a threat grimace. There are extended bouts of fanning, usually with the right hand, sometimes the left, with a frequency of three to four flaps per second. The bouts are interrupted by intense staring at the top of the spread hand held at arm's length. John has no articulate speech but laughs, cries, croons and engages in extended bouts of voiceless oral sounds. He is indifferent to his peers, absolutely never initiates social contact with them, but immediately and indiscriminately approaches adults to climb into lap or arms.

FIRST IMPRESSIONS

While the orphans are being fed, we return to the refectory for our own noonday meal. It begins exceptionally today, with hors d'oeuvres of herring and tomatoes in mayonnaise, perhaps because it is Ascension Day. On other days, the first course is a thick soup containing finely shredded vegetables. The entree consists of four dishes: potatoes, usually french-fried but sometimes home-fried or mashed; a vegetable, such as cabbage in a white sauce; well-cooked meat in gravy, which we thought at first was mutton but proved to be beef; and finally the national dish, manioc, a tropical plant similar to the American cassava, with a large starchy root. Next come delicious sweet little bananas, small green oranges and a kind of tapioca pudding. The beverage is Primus beer, the largest industry in Burundi and a matter of some national pride. Homemade banana beer is also plentiful, a rather strong alcoholic beverage with a rancid taste made from fermented bananas. The clergy eats well in Burundi, and much of its produce is grown in its own fields.

The typical farmer—90 percent of the population is engaged in subsistence agriculture—is less well off. Despite the abundance of cattle, meat consumption is minimal, for cattle continue to be symbols of wealth and prestige. In any case, the cattle are lean, of poor quality, and give little milk. Since fish is unknown inland, the farmers' diet is low in protein, but high in starch: most meals include beans, manioc or sweet potatoes. As a result, untold thousands of children suffer from the nutritional disease called kwashiorkor. I remember the pitifully thin urchins with distended bellies that we passed in the town square as we drove to the archdiocese.

The sitting area of the refectory is simply furnished. An upholstered bench with cushions covered in a floral print; some wooden chairs and a low table on which are scattered ashtrays and a church newsletter; an old refrigerator; a radio; and some odd pieces of furniture. On the wall are pictures of the pope, an elderly saint, President Micombero in military uniform, Prince Rwagasore in formal wear, and the archbishop himself in ecclesiastic garb with pectoral cross and skullcap. He seems to be about thirty-five in the picture, and cuts a handsome figure, aristocratic and shy.

Richard and I digest our lunch in the sitting area and take stock. We could now at least provisionally rule out most of the remaining hereditary diseases. So far, we can find no signs of the disorders of protein, sugar or lipid metabolism. As I got to know John better, I had to acknowledge that he didn't have the grotesque appearance of gargoylism nor the limb and back deformities that it entails. The possibility of autism was, if anything, enhanced. It was worth reviewing at this point what we knew about it, but we had to admit that that wasn't much. Some lean toward the view that it is a distinct disease, but many psychologists and psychiatrists contend that it is a pattern of symptoms —a syndrome—like mental retardation and not a single disease entity like, say, PKU. From either point of view, John could be both feral and autistic. If autism is a syndrome with many causes, rearing in isolation might be one of them. If autism is a distinct disease, John might indeed have been left in the wild because he suffered from it. To make the diagnosis even trickier, we know that the symptoms of feral rearing and of autism overlap: mutism, for example, is common to both in many cases. So it was just a beginning to class John as autistic—but was he?

Autism has only recently begun to be recognized and described; all the medical, psychological and social advances in its diagnosis and treatment date from the past few decades. In 1943, Leo Kanner, a child psychiatrist at Johns Hopkins University, studied a group of severely disturbed children who had, among other symptoms, a striking indifference to those around them. Borrowing a term from Eugen Bleuler, a Swiss psychiatrist who in 1906 described his psychotic patients as "autistic"—that is, referring everything in the world to themselves— Kanner stated that his child patients had an "autistic disturbance" and introduced the diagnostic label "early infantile autism."

This label puts the child's disturbed emotional ties in the limelight and leaves the perceptual and motor disturbances that accompany them offstage. That may be one reason why early efforts to treat the disease tended to focus on psychoanalysis of parents and child; it was widely believed that autism was the result of noxious mother-child relations. Two developments that fueled this approach were early stud-

Sunday Times

MAGAZINE

April 11, 1976

The boy who thinks he's a monkey

How a real life Tarzan was found in the jungles of Burundi. Doctors say it's a miracle that he's alive.

Out of the wilderness . . . John the Jungle Boy, named after John the Baptist.

Story and picture : David Barritt

Dressed

Human

Treated

Love

THE DEPARTURE

———

A ROADSIDE SCENE

A MARKET IN THE CAPITAL
———
MURAMVYA

A COMPOUND

A PROVINCIAL MARKET

THE GITEGA ORPHANAGE

FATHER TUHABONYE (LEFT) AND JOHN

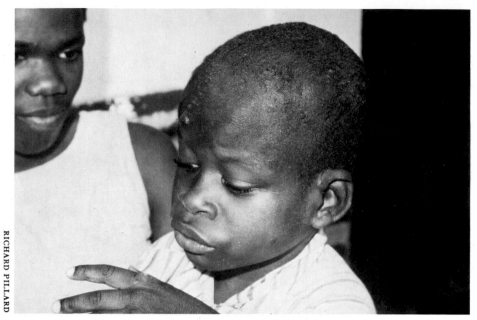

JOHN

JOHN

KIGANDA MISSION

HARLAN AT DAVID KAEUPER'S

ies reporting that the families of autistic children had above-average social class and IQs, and Bruno Bettelheim's moving book of case studies, *The Empty Fortress: Infantile Autism and the Birth of the Self,* in which he traces autism to unconscious parental hostility and rejection. In those days parents of autistic children carried a heavy load of guilt; no doubt some buckled under it and were hostile and rejecting at times, or worse. But later studies revealed no difference in class or IQ between the parents of autistic children and those of nonautistic children when extraneous variables are suitably controlled. (For example, more educated parents are more likely to bring their autistic child to a specialist for diagnosis.) Further studies analyzed the families of autistic children, their neuroses, their emotional demonstrativeness and responsiveness, their ways of communicating with their children, and found nothing to link the home environment with autism.

Currently, this psychogenic explanation of autism is out of vogue, and more attention is given to the perceptual and motor disturbances of the autistic child, on the theory that these disturbances may be the cause of his language and social disorders, or at least share with them a common source. Perceptually, the autistic child does not seem to receive an adequate flow of stimulation from his environment, and he* engages in activities that, on the face of it, are an attempt to compensate. He will often fail to react to verbal commands or sounds, as John failed to react to the sound of the tuning fork or to learn to react to his name. He may not startle in response to sudden loud noises (although John did). The autistic child often seems to use peripheral vision, as John does, and he may not respond visually to new objects in the environment, just as John failed to fixate on us or the little red ball or other things we gave him.

Objects placed in the autistic child's hand may fall away, as they did with John. He may not respond to painful stimuli, although John did respond to our pinprick. In one interesting experiment, autistic children were matched with mentally retarded children of the same IQ,

---

*Since four times as many males as females are autistic, I use the masculine pronoun *he* to refer to the autistic child.

and both groups were taught to respond for food when a light and noise came on together. Then the children were tested with the light alone and the noise alone. The retarded children, like normal children, responded equally to both parts of the original stimulus. But the autistic children responded only to one or the other part. When the autistic child was confronted with the part he had failed to respond to—say, the light—the physiological measures, such as heart rate, took the same little leap then as they did when the light and noise were presented on the very first trial. In other words, despite his training, he acted as if he had never seen one of the two stimuli before.

Another study showed that autistic children do not seem to get normal stimulation from their sense of balance—the vestibular organ. When you whirl around and then stop, your eyes involuntarily rotate in the opposite direction. This reflex is called vestibular nystagmus, and autistic children show less of it than normal children when spun around in a lighted room. Interestingly, we spun John repeatedly and could not detect any nystagmus. Also, autistic children are atypical with respect to the senses of taste and smell. The autistic child may favor these "proximal" senses to explore his environment over the more "distal" senses of vision and hearing. Moreover, he may have unusual food preferences, as indeed John does.

Perhaps because few stimuli from the environment are getting through, the autistic child seems to generate some of his own. He may rub, bang or flick his ears or bang his head. He may whirl, rock back and forth, or roll his head around, stimulating his senses of balance and of movement. Likewise, he may flap his hand back and forth in front of his eyes, providing visual stimulation. He may scrutinize details; he may have bouts of intense staring. The autistic child may engage in self-destructive activities, thus providing himself with painful stimuli. Head-banging and hand-biting are particularly common, especially in the more retarded autistic child. John shows most of these symptoms. His forehead is callused from striking it with his hands and from banging his head against such objects as his crib. His wrists are callused from his habit of gnawing on them. The tips of his ears are callused, although we have not seen him strike them. He constantly flaps his hand in front of his eyes and will stop occasionally to stare fixedly at his hand held out at arm's length. But most striking of all among his self-stimulating activities is his incessant chattering, which causes his tongue and cheeks to vibrate and create a loud sound. An autistic child may be made highly agitated by a sudden change in his environment, such as a loud noise, a change in illumination, a rough fabric, or a ride in an elevator or car. John doesn't seem to mind car rides or being whirled around, but he does indeed become hysterical when his eyes are covered, and he has a strong aversion to having his head touched.

The most typical motor disturbances in autism involve the hands and arms. Hand-flapping some three to four times a second is a very common symptom—nearly three-fourths of the autistic children in one sample showed it. The child's gait may also be disturbed, and toe walking is a common finding. John has both these symptoms. Other motor disturbances include rocking, swaying and head-banging, and John displays all three from time to time.

The autistic child may acquire no speech or language, or he may stop somewhere along the way in normal development. When he does have language, it is usually not communicative; instead, the child merely echoes what is said to him. Those few children who do develop communicative language generally speak without inflection and without conveying emotion for the rest of their lives. Autism and mental retardation go together. Although some autistic children may have a normal IQ or improve in mental age in later development, most—perhaps three-fourths—are permanently retarded. There seems to be a consensus among psychiatrists that if an autistic child has not acquired language by the age of five, he will always be grossly retarded and disturbed. John clearly is retarded.

Beyond his disturbances of perception, movement and language, the autistic child is also out of contact with the social world around him. The reason may be that if he can't remember facial features, if he can't talk, if he's busily engaged in some stereotyped or self-abusive activity, he is hardly in a position to develop good social relations. In any case, we expect a lack of relating to peers, poor eye contact, no social smile, no response to being picked up or even aversion to physical contact, disinterest in games, anxiety with strangers, intermittent responsiveness to parents. Bouts of laughing, giggling, crying and screaming without apparent cause are also common. John has most of these symptoms, although he seems to take to strangers rather well.

It is difficult to distinguish autism from schizophrenia, developmental aphasia and maternal deprivation, but John didn't seem to fit the pattern of any of these last three disorders exclusively. Children with aphasia are late in understanding and producing spoken language, but they engage in nonverbal communication, gesturing and pointing, of which we saw none with John. There is no reason to expect fanning, bouts of staring, and toe gait in aphasia. Similarly, these symptoms, as well as John's averted gaze, are not characteristic of children who have suffered maternal deprivation. On the other hand, given the attention John was receiving in Gitega, a deprived child would play games and would make some progress in language. Childhood schizophrenia alone would not lead us to expect John's utter lack of language, sensory and motor disorders, and severe inability to learn. All in all, we were disinclined toward the hereditary and developmental disorders, save autism. John is an autistic child or a feral child, or conceivably both.

There were several tests Richard and I wanted to carry out in Bujumbura, laboratory tests that would be routine in the States but were difficult or impossible here. Above all, I was hoping we could get the electroencephalograph to work. An EEG, a brain-wave machine, is a complicated piece of electronic apparatus, although its principle of operation is straightforward. The brain is composed of millions of nerve cells, neurons, which like fine electric wires, finer than a strand of spiderweb, transmit minute amounts of electrical energy, on the order of several millionths of a volt. When an electrical impulse travels down a nerve, a minute magnetic field is created; if hundreds of thousands of nerves are conducting at once in some region of the brain, their tiny magnetic fields summate and the activity can be detected on the corresponding area of the scalp. The EEG, a super-sensitive voltmeter, detects this electrical activity. One pole of the EEG "plug" is placed on the scalp over the brain region of interest; the other can be placed on a "ground" or neutral region, such as the earlobe. An electrical potential will be detected, but it must be amplified enormously if it is to drive the pen of the recorder and leave a permanent record of ink on paper. Amplifying those minute electric potentials is the same sort of problem as making concert-hall sound from the minute vibrations in the groove of a stereo record.

The big problem with the EEG is to determine what is going on inside the brain from electrodes pasted in various positions on the scalp. There are many relay stations—nuclei—carefully packed in the brain, each one sending cables of neurons to the others. Something important could be wrong yet buried in that buzz of electrical activity. It's like trying to detect a bad circuit at telephone central from outside the building.

Brain-wave tests are especially useful in detecting various types of epilepsy because often there are characteristic rhythmic electrical discharges specific to the type of epilepsy. An epileptic focus can be determined by noting in what part of the brain the abnormal discharges begin. If John's hand-flapping is a symptom of epilepsy, as Zarotchintsev thinks, there is a pretty good chance of seeing it. If, on the contrary, he has brain damage from infectious disease, congenital injury or metabolic error, we'll probably just see signs of diffuse injury not specific to any particular part of the brain or to any particular disease.

Richard described some research his colleagues at Boston University Medical School are conducting. They are tackling the problem of brain dysfunction by inserting electrodes directly into the brain— electrodes so microscopically fine that they can record the activity of a single neuron. Of course, this is only done on animals. A good operator can drop an electrode though a rat's skull and hit a neucleus the size of a pinhead.

In addition to the EEG, Richard wanted X-rays. Skull X-rays would help rule out a variety of brain diseases that would leave their trace on the films as well as in John's behavior: fractures of the skull; defects in its shape, the cranial anomalies; growths or anomalies in the formation of the brain. Bone X-rays would help determine his age and preclude the remote possibility that his peculiar gait was due to some abnormality in bone structure. They would also serve as a check on metabolic disorders and infectious diseases that affect bone growth.

Third, a blood sample was necessary. Back in Boston, John's blood would be checked for evidence of several hereditary diseases, including the disorders of protein metabolism. There is some intriguing evidence that autistic children have abnormally high levels of serotonin in their blood. Serotonin is one of the chemicals in the body that carries messages from one nerve cell to the next. It is one of a group of neurotransmitters that are found in areas of the brain that control emotions and behavior. Serotonin is derived by enzymes from an amino acid, tryptophan, that cannot be manufactured in the body and must be supplied in the diet. Hence a defect in the control of the enzyme that converts tryptophan to serotonin may be a cause or a consequence of autism. If John has elevated blood serotonin, it would support a diagnosis of autism. Then, too, we would want to check John's blood for various current diseases: infection, infestation by parasites, anemia.

Fourth, a urine sample and a stool sample should be collected. From an analysis of John's urine we could tell if there were errors of protein, carbohydrate or lipid metabolism, frequently associated with mental retardation. Amino acid molecules from our diet are linked together into protein molecules necessary for life. This linking process is managed by other proteins, called enzymes. Some people are born lacking one or another enzyme, so the amino acids are linked improperly. These "alien" products of metabolism are excreted into the urine.

"Looking at his stool under the microscope will reveal the eggs of parasites," Richard explained. "I learned about them in medical school and remember most of the names—*Wuchereria bancrofti, Schistosoma mansoni, Dracuncula medinensis,* but I've never seen a case. Well, this may be the chance; but parasites aren't a cause of mental retardation and certainly not of what has happened to John."

Finally, there were a variety of observations we wanted to make that are difficult to carry out with any active young child, but proved impossible with one as active as John. He wouldn't let us touch his head, and yet we needed to look in his ears to be sure that there were no external signs of ear disease that would give a simple explanation to his apparent hearing loss. It was unlikely, but he might even have a perforated eardrum as a result of some ear infection, like our monk of the other evening. Although John would never let us look him straight in the eye, that's just what we wanted to do with the ophthalmoscope, a light beam and system of lenses that make it possible to look through the pupil of the eye to see the blood vessels and the retina within. A glance at the light-sensitive film of skin on the rear wall of his eye, his retina, could possibly yield a simple explanation of his averted gaze: perhaps the center of this film had lost its light-sensitive material and John's only way of seeing clearly was to look at what he wanted to see with the side of his eye. Spotting of the retina would also point back to the metabolic disorders, including the fabled Laurence-Moon-Biedl syndrome. Moreover, we could detect evidence there of other diseases. We were especially interested in looking in John's mouth and throat for any flaw that might be hampering his speech; for example, a cleft palate or a paralyzed vocal cord. We wanted to photograph his body close up from head to foot and to make the 16mm films we had promised the networks.

We needed and wanted all these things—EEG, X-rays, body fluids, close-up examination—for ourselves, it is true, to find any evidence of brain disease or of life in the wild, but we also wanted them for John: an infection, a malformed bone, a ruptured eardrum, or a metabolic disorder might be treatable. Epilepsy is treatable, and so are tumors and nutritional deficiencies. John would have to be taken back to the hospital in Bujumbura for the tests. We returned to the orphanage to explain our reasoning to Sister Nestor and to ask her permission.

It is dark by six in the tropics. The children are finishing dinner and getting ready for bed. It was interesting for us to watch what was happening. The tiny orphans—there are about two dozen of them, ranging in age from about six months to six years—were playing simple games and singing "Frère Jacques" by themselves and later with adults. Those only two or three years old would join in the group with perfect composure. There was an unusual sense of everyone doing everything together and not, as would happen in a comparable group of American children, fighting, crying and running about. These children seemed well behaved in an almost uncanny way. They would go up to adults, gravely shake hands and say *"Bonjour,"* yet they never seemed to be disciplined by adults nor did they seem the least tense or unhappy. The children seemed not to be individuals at all, but to be a group of Lilliputians playing, singing and going to bed without a whimper.

Against this peaceful background, John was running about and vocalizing, but the others calmly accepted his behavior. At times the staff would deal him into one of the circle games. He would hold hands with an adult on one side and a child on the other and would dance around for a while, then would break away and resume his chattering and fanning. We wondered whether our examination that day had upset him, as he seemed so active, but Sister Nestor told us that he was generally this active in the evenings. Occasionally we saw John attend when adults called him. We watched the group being put to bed while we discussed with Nestor and Petronille the desirability of going to Bujumbura on the following morning. They both agreed that Father Tuhabonye would have the final say in the matter and that we must consult with him.

During dinner, I noticed that the cooks had been taking furtive glances through the kitchen door at their unusual guests; the meal over, I asked if we could pay our compliments to the chef. The kitchen is about twelve feet square with one small sink and an ancient stove fueled by charcoal. Smoke filled the room, and everything was black with soot. There were kettles and serving dishes of metal, but some of the utensils were handmade of wood. The whole kitchen was in complete clutter. There were four cooks, and we heard from two of them about their lives, about how long they had worked for the archbishop, and about their children.

Father Melchior took us to his apartment to call Zarotchintsev and make arrangements for tomorrow. Clean and neat, the apartment was decorated with some African artifacts, such as woven baskets and a spear on the wall. The Burundi telephone book is a masterpiece of unhelpfulness. For one thing, it was issued in 1973 and many of the phone numbers have since been changed. We could find neither Bartoli's number nor Zarotchintsev's, and it was not possible to get Information. Eventually we gave up.

FIRST IMPRESSIONS

By nine the other priests had returned from the consecration of a new chapel in Gitega and we sat down to have a talk, particularly with Father Tuhabonye. We reported on the studies that we had done so far. We proposed taking John to Bujumbura the next day, which would require them to let us borrow their favorite orphan, a member of the orphanage staff, Petronille (who also happens to be Tuhabonye's secretary), a large car for all of us and our luggage, and of course, a driver. Tuhabonye said something like "Damn it, I had a lot of work for Petronille to do tomorrow," but he immediately acquiesced to everything we asked.

VI

FURTHER
TESTS

FRIDAY, MAY 28—BUJUMBURA
From Richard's diary

Up at six-thirty, overcast sky with heavy rain. We had coffee at the refectory and learned from Pierre that the total budget for the orphanage, including the care of twenty-five or thirty children and the staff of eight, comes to less than $5,000 a year. Of this, $1,500 is raised by the wife of President Micombero.

Promptly at seven as promised, a van and driver appeared. Kaeuper had told us that it takes forever to get anything done because Burundians have no sense of time. But they have certainly clicked it off for us. Pierre decided to keep Petronille after all and sent two other girls from the orphanage—Maria Theresa and the beautiful Justine, whose picture I took yesterday with the Polaroid. Just before we left, Pierre thought of lunch and immediately had a bag of bananas and bread made up for us. "You certainly won't want to bother to stop for it." This thoughtful kindness was completely in character for everyone we have met here.

Off we go, John fanning and vocalizing but at least not trying to jump out of the van. I sat in front with the Nikon hoping for opportunities to take pictures. Despite the heavy rain there were always people walking along the roadside, most of them bearing loads in the tightly woven baskets on their heads. Some of the women had ancient umbrellas; some carried the huge fronds of the banana palm over their heads to deflect the water; most just resigned themselves to getting soaked. They looked uncomfortable. We saw a man washing himself and his clothing under a little waterfall spilling over a hillside. We met an army convoy, perhaps fifteen trucks camouflaged with fresh-cut branches. Each was packed with tall soldiers armed with rifles. A glossy blue Mercedes whipped past, with several white middle-aged ladies, smartly dressed, sitting in the back. Who could they possibly be?

Most often people stared at us with curiosity. If we waved and smiled, they generally waved back. They were shy about being photographed, and that made me shy about taking pictures. Uniformly, they appeared a quiet, sober people, the nature of whose existence we could, even now, barely imagine. The huts of Bujumbura appear in the distance. We're back in civilization!

Prince Regent Charles Clinic is made up of a score of small buildings separated by grassy lots and connected by covered concrete walkways. People swarmed everywhere. In the lots, the relatives of the sick camp out to provide nursing care. Some parents were encouraging their crippled son to walk with the aid of his crutches. Others were inspecting dressings and cleaning wounds. More were gathered in small groups chatting, stoking fires, preparing food. Most of the buildings house crowded wards, all on the same plan. Twenty metal beds in a row on the left, twenty metal beds in a row on the right, a narrow aisle in between. We edged our way along the crowded walkway, through outpatients lined up for medical attention, and found Zarotchintsev in his office reading a Russian paperback, *Undercover Pentagon.* He led us into one of his wards. Some forty patients sat about in various postures chattering incoherently or lay staring vacantly. The iron cots are practically touching. Many patients lay on the steel springs; other beds had a few rags or an old blanket to serve as a mattress. "Psychotics look like psychotics everywhere," I volunteered.

"I don't see much depressive illness, mostly schizophrenia. It's very hard. I'm the only psychiatrist for six million people, if you count the border areas of Zaire and Tanzania. The patients refuse to take pills and prefer herbal remedies, so I have to give drugs by injection. But I don't have nearly enough. Every now and then I get a box of miscellaneous drugs from Moscow—often things I can't really use."

"No linen, no equipment?"

"Occasionally we get a sheet, but the patients steal it. There's an electroshock apparatus, but I don't use it much any more. That's out of vogue in the States, too, isn't it? And there's an electroencephalograph that's been broken as long as anyone can remember. A pity, because I've done research on brain waves in Moscow."

We wanted to get some 16mm film of John before we began the tests, so we had Maria Theresa lead him up and down the field behind the hospital to demonstrate his unusual gait. After a few passes he started to limp. It was strange to see his response; he was obviously in pain, but he did not stop or hold his foot or search for the thorn that Justine quickly found there. It was as though he was not able to associate the pain with the appropriate place on his body.

Back to Zarotchintsev's office. A Murundi approaches with some X-rays, which Zarotchintsev holds up to the sunlight. In French, "Look at that! Multiple fractures of the skull. This man's wife will die; but what can you do?" In Kirundi, "I'll look at her in the morning." The man politely withdrew.

Zarotchintsev leads us to the X-ray laboratory; a score of people are queued up quietly on the loggia in front of a locked door. A soldier is lying on the ground on a stretcher, moaning; his pants have been removed and his right leg is covered with blood and dirt from his knee to his ankle. He starts to jabber loudly, repeating some phrase in Kirundi; perhaps he is entreating us; he looks terrified. No one seems to notice; they are not looking away, merely not looking. I am acutely uncomfortable, but what can you do? Then I realize with disgust that I have used Zarotchintsev's phrase. He knocks on the laboratory door; there is a rapid exchange in Kirundi; and we are admitted to a stage set from a Frankenstein movie. The cavernous room is dimly lit; huge cables are strung everywhere; electrical equipment, obviously in disrepair, is stacked along the walls of the room, covered with dust. A half-dozen aides are milling about. It is oppressively hot and close.

We have sedated John with a 10-milligram shot of Valium, but he is in no mood to be X-rayed. He writhes, screams and flails when we try to position him on the table. We are all sweating profusely in the tropical damp. Tempers are rising, and commands fly back and forth in Kirundi, French, and English. You stand at the button. *Prenez vous deux la jambe gauche*—the left leg! Hold him. You two take the right. You two take his shoulders. (Harlan and I took his head.) Now, go! We quickly get six films. It is possible to overpower a ten-year-old boy; it's a question of numbers.

Later I realized that the X-ray technicians, most of them young women in training, were not wearing the lead aprons or lead-impregnated gloves that are regulation in radiology labs everywhere. Nor did they have the little badge monitors that detect accidental exposure to stray radiation. Radiation is cumulative and can cause birth defects, even cancer, but resources here are too desperately precious to buy protection.

On the way back to Zarotchintsev's office, a nurse recognized John. She is Elizabeth Noigenegene, who was quoted in the Barritt article and who had cared for John during his days as a patient here. It was interesting to see, as she spoke to him and tried to pick him up, that he showed not the least sign of recognizing her.

John was calm when I reached the office, so I conducted a routine physical examination. Pulse 104. Pressure 110 over 70. Respiration rate 16. Lungs clear. Tiny inguinal lymph nodes. Belly soft and slightly distended. Soft systolic murmur best heard over the cardiac apex close to the sternum. Back and arms free of scars, eczema. Good fingernails, palms normally creased, knuckles callused, wrists rugated, ulnar calluses (from biting), fine normal skin. One-inch scar on the crown of the head; one and three-eighths inch scar to the left of midline over the occiput, one round scar, one-half inch in diameter, behind right ear. Thickened callused skin between bridge of nose and hairline. One-inch scar under right eye. Small scar inside of right ear, and some callusing on top of outer ears, which are normally shaped. Feet smooth, well-formed, no callus, no eczema. Testes about the size of a peanut, penis normal, ready erection. Abdominal reflex normal. Left knee jerk (no right elicited). Responds to serrated wheel at extremities. No response to cotton strokes. Withdraws sharply from the scent of amyl acetate. Difficult to examine mouth: maxillary and mandibular tongue ordinary. Three molars, top and bottom. Good visual tracking of the flashlight. Much less lateral gaze than we have seen previously.

Hot and tired, I tried repeatedly to get a good look in John's ears and mouth, but without success. We put two drops of cyclogel in his eyes to dilate his pupils, and for the next quarter of an hour I assumed various bizarre postures trying to glimpse the inside of John's eyes. The sudden sneak attack seemed to work best, and finally I got a tantalizing glance. There seemed to be a blotch of pigment on John's retina. The entire view through the ophthalmoscope lasted only a fraction of a second, but that was enough to convince us that a more adequate examination must be performed. Pigmentation on the retina can be a sign of retinitis pigmentosa, a hereditary disease that destroys vision progressively over a period of years, working from the center of the eye outward. Could this explain why John is always looking off to the side? Peripheral vision may be all he has left!

After giving John some more Valium, I went in search of the hospital ophthalmologist. He dilated John's eyes further, and while waiting for the drug to take effect, we went by the lab to pick up the X-rays. To our amateur view, they were normal. We could see John's teeth clearly, and from their number and state of eruption, he must be ten or eleven years old, though at a glance he would strike you as a six-year-old.

Harlan introduced himself to the hospital administrator and asked to see the electroencephalograph, which was stowed in a corner of his office under a sheet of plastic. It is a rather old and cumbersome piece of equipment, but Harlan's hopes rose when he saw that the line cord had no plug. Closer inspection revealed that there was no recording paper and no ink, but what made the situation really hopeless was that the headpiece and electrode leads had also disappeared. Harlan got down on the floor and copied the model and serial numbers. One bright spot: it was manufactured in Paris. We promised to get the missing parts and the manual on the way back to the United States.

In the ophthalmologist's office, John seemed frightened (by his dilated pupils, I think) and exhausted, but despite the heavy sedation, he was screaming, struggling and resisting with amazing tenacity. The Belgian doctor had an ingenious device suited to the purpose: a reflecting ophthalmoscope, a slit lamp with two lenses, one held near his own eye, one near the child's. This gave him more leeway to focus on the moving eye, and he could keep his face far from John's, but nothing would do, John wanted out, and finally we tried pinning him down while a technician held his eyelids open. This was no more successful, as the one thing we couldn't do was hold his eyeballs still, but the good doctor had a solution for that, too. Knock him out.

I would dearly have loved to. I had had it with the day-long battle. I was hot, dirty, hungry (we had even skipped Pierre's banana and bread lunch) and tired: we had been going since six A.M., it was now four, the EEG was broken, we couldn't get a one-second look in his eye, the hospital was closing up for the day, we still had the blood tests to do, and I knew what John would think about that. Put him to sleep and everyone would be happier all around. But anesthetizing a child with injectable drugs is a dangerous procedure without an anesthesiologist at hand. I wouldn't want to be anesthetized at the Prince Regent Charles Clinic, and neither would you. So John wasn't either.

The director of the blood lab, a distinguished-looking, self-assured Belgian with an unbending manner, listened courteously as we explained the reason for our visit. He seemed distinctly unimpressed, whether by the sight of the two bedraggled Americans in front of him or by Harlan's French (which Harlan said had capitulated to fatigue), I couldn't tell. Perhaps it was the prospect of another patient at closing time late on a Friday afternoon. "Put the boy on the table," he said, as if that were the simplest matter in the world. We braced ourselves for another struggle. With John pinned, an assistant tried to draw blood and repeatedly failed. The doctor stepped in and probed both arms time and again, but without success. Finally in disgust he pricked John's finger, smeared the blood on a few slides, and we all left.

The best drink I have ever had was the rum and coke I drank in David Kaeuper's house a little while later. John had returned with his guardians and chauffeur to Gitega. Harlan and I were sprawled on David's couch listening to the silence and feeling the cool breeze filtering through the living room. "You can go weeks without food, a week without sleep, but only a day or two without water," I said, swizzling the ice cubes in my drink with a finger.

"How long can you go without a bath?" Harlan asked.

"Another five minutes."

Just then the zamu broke in; sputtering unintelligible French—or was it Kirundi?—he said something about a taxi and insisted that we follow him.

I had no idea what the problem was or how I would deal with it in English, but I followed him across Kaeuper's spacious lawn, across the dirt road, and into the garden of a completely charming house. At the front door I found an attractive, vivacious woman in her early thirties; she appeared dressed for an evening in Paris, not Bujumbura. Her hair was arranged, her make-up was sparingly but carefully applied, and she was wearing a green evening gown.

"I'm Elsa Vloothuis." This was said in the British accent Americans always find distinguished.

"I'm Richard Pillard."

We both laughed at the unexpectedness of our meeting and the contrast in our appearances; I had obviously just come out of the bush. She could no more understand the zamu than I, but he seemed satisfied and left. I explained why Harlan and I were at David's, and she invited us for drinks in an hour's time.

A while later we sat on the patio sipping the gin and tonics that Jules Vloothuis had served from behind a bar. A handsome middle-aged man with wavy blond hair, penetrating blue eyes and an aquiline nose, he seemed more reserved than his wife. In charmingly accented English, he explained that he had traveled East Africa for many years as the representative of a Brussels export-import firm, and had been stationed in Burundi some three years ago.

"It's very nice, you know, the comforts and all," I heard Elsa say as my gaze wandered over the vast luxurious gardens that extended from the terrace down the hill toward the city. I could see the scattered lights of Bujumbura below and beyond the faint outline of the shore of Lake Tanganyika. "But it's a frightful bore. The servants take care of the house and cooking, we have a nanny for the youngest child, and then the gardeners for the grounds."

"They must need supervision."

"Oh, today I went with them to get some bushes for the corner of the lawn where the driveway begins. It needs something . . . And I shop for vegetables with cook. But there's really nothing to do. Play tennis with other Belgians—the Americans stick quite to themselves, you know, and the Russians live in a shabby housing development and never go out. Then the yacht club for lunch. Horseback riding in the afternoon. Our oldest, Marie-José, has started lessons. Parties in the evening. Always the same people. One knows everybody. Occasionally, the French cultural center will show a bad film. It's really impossible.

"You live for the three months' leave every two years," she continued, getting up to freshen her drink. "A chance to see what's going on in the world. The new styles. I come back with trunks full of dresses, don't I, dear." She gave Jules a peck on the cheek. "Once I'm in Brussels, I don't want to come back, of course, but what can you do? I can't stay there and become a *hausfrau,* raise three children in a four-room flat, do the ironing and the cooking. I'd hardly be happier like that, would I? But tell us about you. Do you think the boy's really a monkey child?"

I put the same question to Harlan a half-hour later over dinner at the San Pierre Restaurant on the shores of Lake Tanganyika. Elsa and Jules had recommended it; like their home, it was large, expensive-looking and just a little showy, and it had an excellent view. The menu featured fish from the lake at a price any Burundian could afford—if he saved all his income for four months. There was one other couple. Our waiter, a tall, very thin black man dressed in white with eye-catching gold bracelets, arranged the table setting while the disco tune "Fly, Robin, Fly" played in the background.

"Do you think he could still be feral, Harlan? The physical and neurological exam didn't turn up any new symptoms. The X-rays are not clearly abnormal. The chances are less than ever that he started life with any metabolic disorder I know of, or any flaw in brain or skull structure, or any infectious disease like maternal rubella or syphilis. Though I wonder about that spot on his retina that I might have seen. We'll have to take a closer look, get more blood, and do the EEGs."

"So let's say we drop the first hypothesis except for autism. To check that out as well as childhood diseases we trace his history. That's what we do next."

"We find the soldiers. I've always wanted to see the beautiful southwest."

"Let's work back. For the past year he's been in the orphanage at Gitega. That takes us to June 1975. For the three years preceding, he was in the insane ward. Admitted in June of '72. From the orphanage in Bujumbura."

"We pick up the trail there."

When we left the restaurant, Harlan and I sought out our friend Bartoli at the compound of the World Health Organization and accepted his invitation to review our progress and plans over a drink. His home was more modest than the Vloothuises' but quite comfortable and attractively furnished. His stunning French wife, Colette, was at the door to meet us with a daughter of ten or eleven, a younger boy, and two enormous Great Danes.

We recounted what had happened since the morning—could it be only four days ago?—that we arrived and he introduced us to Zarotchintsev.

We're forming the opinion that John was either autistic or feral or both. We can't get the electroencephalograph to work and we're not enthusiastic about anesthetizing John at the Prince Regent Charles

FURTHER TESTS

Clinic in order to draw blood and conduct a complete physical.

"My dear friends," said Bartoli, "I agree with you, it would be risky. You see what it's like here. My maternity ward has thirty pair of sheets for eighty beds. And we're rich. At one time we had none. When I came, the hospital generator was broken, so there were no lights and we couldn't perform surgery. There was an enormous barrel standing in the yard for months and months. No one had any idea what it was for. It turned out to be an autoclave run by gas. Now we use it to sterilize everything, and we hang wet laundry around it so we have a drying room. Look, adhesive tape is so scarce, when I change a dressing I remove the tape carefully, put on a new gauze pad, and replace the tape. I got a package of sutures from Italy last week; I drove home and locked it in my desk."

"Isn't the World Health Organization helping?" I asked.

"They're interested in preventive, not curative, medicine. I have no antibiotics or analgesics. Oh yes, I have four vials of Valium I keep locked in my desk. Listen, the World Health Organization launched a campaign against body lice: four hundred thousand dollars. The lice carry typhus, which is very common here; our own son had it. They bought enough louse powder to cover every man, woman and child. What happened? People don't own a change of clothing, so after the treatment they simply became reinfested. At one time a herbicide was distributed for use on the coffee plants. The workers used the herbicide on themselves to kill the lice, but the chemical got in their blood and they got sick. You see? What can you do?"

"Why don't the Americans help?" Harlan asked. "We haven't seen a single American doctor. Russians, Belgians, Italians, but not Americans."

"The Americans! They promised sixty thousand dollars' worth of relief effort. Do you imagine what that is for the States, or compared to the needs here? What is sixty thousand dollars? Nothing! That was six years ago, six years, and not a penny has been released. But of course they're pouring money into Kenya: that's in the Western sphere of influence."

How can we complete John's tests while we try and piece together his history? The solution to our dilemma hit all of us at about the same moment. We would take John to Nairobi, where the rest of the tests we needed could be carried out in proper hospital facilities. But this solution presented new problems in turn. Could we get permission for the boy to leave the country? Bartoli suggested that we ask Dr. Deogratias Barakamfitiye, the chief physician in Gitega whom the governor had proposed we meet, to accompany us to Nairobi. If he agreed, he could probably secure the visas. But then we didn't have the funds to fly four of us to Nairobi and back—about eight hundred dollars. Colette suggested we ask for the President's helicopter, which had just flown overhead. I thought of an air taxi; there's one that operates out of Mombasa in Kenya, but a phone call revealed that the cost would be a thousand dollars. I suggested Harlan call the American embassy and ask for an air force plane. After all, the ambassador promised to help and it would be a good public relations gesture. He called and was politely told that there were no American planes in the area. Suddenly Bartoli had the answer. If we put Nairobi off to the end of our stay, Harlan and I would not have to return. We could have our tickets rewritten to go to Boston via Nairobi, and the only expense would be ferrying the doctor and child there and back. Agreed. We would continue our efforts to trace John's history, picking up the trail at the Bujumbura orphanage. When we reached the end of that trail, we would all fly to Nairobi.

SATURDAY, MAY 29—BUJUMBURA

At breakfast, Richard and I assaulted David with anger that had scarcely attenuated during the night. Why, in the face of disease and suffering at every turn in Burundi, were the Americans doing nothing? Why, if Bartoli was telling it straight, did it take six years to release a mere $60,000? First, David replied, the Burundi government is anti-American. They vote against the United States on every issue brought before the United Nations. Their anti-Israel vote caused the United States to stop the $60,000 self-help project, but the funds were finally unfrozen. The money has been available for nearly a year, only a contractor's estimates are needed to collect it, and no one can get the paperwork together. According to David, this is the problem: the Barundi lack initiative. The Americans shipped a $7,500 blood lab for the clinic at Ibuye, but nothing came of it until an Englishman took charge. Another example: the German government gave ten scholarships in economics. The Barundi refused to issue visas because six of those chosen were Rwanda refugees and only four were Burundi Batutsi. The military gets 25 percent of the $30,000,000 national budget, the Ministry of Health, 6 1/2 percent—and most of that is spent in Bujumbura on officials and civil servants. And then there's the Tutsi-Hutu conflict. Hundreds of thousands slaughtered in 1965, '69, and '72. How can you help a government that is willing to do that to its people? "It is rumored that Hutu priests took refuge in the archdiocese of Gitega, and your fine friends there turned them over to the Batutsi. You see what I mean? What can you do?"

David left pleading an urgent appointment. It was only weeks later that I read Roger Morris's chronicle of American indifference, inertia and irresponsibility during the genocide in Burundi and learned some of the things we might have done. The killing that took place, during a four-month period in the summer of 1972, at the rate of a thousand men, women and children a day had its roots in the long history of tribal rivalry between the Batutsi and the Bahutu. The rivalry goes back some three centuries, as Pierre Smith had told us, to the period when the Batutsi migrated down the Nile and into the lake region of central Africa, where they found the Bahutu engaged in small-scale agriculture.

The more recent tribal conflict, however, dates back to the time of Stanley and Livingstone and the colonization of East Africa by the Germans. Burundi was among the last areas of Africa to be penetrated by Europeans; its isolation, difficult terrain and hostile inhabitants discouraged early adventurers and explorers. At the Conference of Berlin, in 1885, it was declared a German area of influence, and within a decade, the Germans had constructed a military station in Bujumbura, hoping for profitable commerce. Belgian victories over Germany in World War I led to its military takeover in Rwanda-Urundi just as a new king, Mwambutsa IV, became monarch at the age of two. The Belgians hoped to use the territory as a pawn: they would cede it to Great Britain; the British would cede a portion of German East Africa to Portugal; the Portuguese would cede their area of the Congo to Belgium. In the end, the Portuguese were not amenable to the barter, but the Allies awarded Rwanda-Urundi to Belgium and the League of Nations declared it a mandate territory under Belgian supervision. The Belgians ruled the country through the mwami, Mwambutsa IV, and the baganwa, who ruled the three dozen chiefdoms and five hundred subchiefdoms under the king. The Belgians tried to train the baganwa and lesser Tutsi chiefs to take up civil service jobs. Otherwise, education was left to the Catholic mission schools. Exploration turned up few mineral resources, so the efforts to raise the subsistence economy focused on agriculture; the most successful move was the introduction of the coffee crop in the 1930's.

After World War II, Rwanda-Urundi was made a UN trust territory—still under Belgian rule—and in 1961 limited self-government was established. King Mwambutsa's eldest son, Ganwa Louis Rwagasore, had married a Muhutu and won the UN-supervised election by a landslide. Within a month after becoming prime minister, he was assassinated. His party then split along ethnic lines, with a Tutsi prince, son-in-law of the mwami, opposing the party leader, a Hutu. Civil disorders broke out. A year later Rwanda became independent through a Hutu coup d'état, and 20,000 Batutsi were killed in a selective genocide. Some 100,000 Batutsi fled across the border into Burundi. The mwami had reason to fear a similar coup not only from the Bahutu but also from the restive Batutsi, who found him an obstacle to their gaining control of government. In 1964, the king removed the Hutu leadership, only to find that their Tutsi successors, who had formed close ties with the Chinese Communists in an effort to topple the pro-Western government, were shipping arms into the country. The king dismissed the new government and reappointed the former minister, a Mahutu, who was promptly assassinated by a refugee from Rwanda employed at the U.S. embassy. In the ensuing election, the Bahutu made substantial gains, which the king sought to minimize by centralizing power under the crown.

FURTHER TESTS

In the fall of 1965, the Hutu-dominated gendarmerie launched an abortive coup d'état. Loyal forces in the predominantly Tutsi army, led by Captain Michel Micombero, put down the uprising and launched a wave of reprisals for the Hutu burnings of Tutsi huts in the province of Muramvya. The American embassy was suspected of complicity in the coup and expelled. The king had fled to Switzerland. The nineteen-year-old crown prince, Charles Ndizeye, deposed his father, dismissed the government, suspended the constitution, and began rule under the dynastic title of Mwami Ntare V. Micombero was appointed prime minister (and minister of defense and of interior). A few months later, while the king was in Kinshasa, Colonel Micombero proclaimed Burundi a republic and himself its president. The administration, education and the army were purged, and the Tutsi reign was unchallenged. A Hutu conspiracy was discovered in 1969 but with the execution of some sixty officers and intellectuals was quickly extinguished.

In late April of 1972, Ntare V asked to return to Burundi as a simple citizen. He had gone to neighboring Uganda for obscure reasons, probably unrelated to tourism. With the loan of a helicopter from the ever-accommodating Idi Amin, Ntare V arrived in Gitega, where he was promptly placed under house arrest in the former palace. Official broadcasts accused him of trying to arrange an invasion of Burundi to reestablish his rule. On April 29, five thousand Bahutu and Mulelists, exiles from Zaire, attacked in the regions of Bujumbura, Gitega and Bururi. Whether the king was implicated may never be known; he was assassinated that night. As the days passed, parts of Bururi province and an area south of Bujumbura remained in rebel hands. By the end of the first week, one to two thousand Batutsi and some three thousand Bahutu were killed. In early May, the Burundi ambassador to the United Nations, appealing for aid to the victims of the fighting, said that fifty thousand persons had been killed. The Americans gave $75,000! Among the dead, according to Barritt's article, were John's parents, while John himself was supposed to have fled onto the forested slopes to the east of Nyanza Lac, in the province of Bururi.

By mid-May, according to one high U.S. official, "we started getting disturbing reports that the government was not just mopping up the rebels but trying to punish the whole Hutu tribe." An American University field team reported that there was systematic extermination of the Hutu elite, including

> the four Hutu members of the [dissolved] cabinet, all the Hutu officers and virtually all the Hutu soldiers in the armed forces; half of Burundi's primary school teachers; and thousands of civil servants, bank clerks, small business men, and domestic servants. At present [August], there is only one Hutu nurse left in the entire country and only a thousand secondary school students survive.

American ambassador Melady had met with President Micombero earlier in the month and had received assurances that undue bloodshed would be avoided. He was instrumental in arranging a letter to the president from the papal nuncio, a low-key document expressing concern. He managed to get some vaccines and bandages shipped in. However pitiful these few efforts, even they were terminated when, in the midst of growing evidence of a major human catastrophe in Burundi, the State Department reassigned Melady in accord with longstanding plans. Official U.S. policy was next to involve the Organization of African Unity, although State well knew that organization's traditional unwillingness to become involved in the internal affairs of its strife-torn members. On May 22, the secretary-general of the OAU visited Burundi and declared solidarity with Micombero. In late June, the OAU Council of Ministers sent Micombero a message supporting the repression: "Thanks to your saving action, peace will be rapidly reestablished, national unity will be consolidated, and territorial integrity will be preserved."

In the face of this pathetic failure of its policy, State launched the third phase of its program of inaction, like the two preceding, an expected failure from the start: it asked various African leaders to intercede. President Jomo Kenyatta of Kenya refused to become involved. President Julius Nyerere of Tanzania could hardly be too effective, since some of the rebels had come over from his country. President Joseph Mobutu of Zaire had previously sent paratroopers at Micombero's request; in any case, he wanted good relations with the Burundi government so that it might deprive Zairean rebels of their sanctuary in Burundi. The president of neighboring Rwanda, a Mahutu, did speak with Micombero, with the expected result.

In late June, the United Nations sent a fact-finding team to Burundi, and on July 4 Secretary-General Waldheim confirmed that the team had found awful suffering and that the dead might number as high as two hundred thousand. The world community scarcely responded. There was a brief outcry in the French National Assembly. The Belgians condemned the genocide and withdrew economic and military aid. No other government raised the issue. Washington was silent.

As the weeks wore on, the trucks loaded with corpses continued to drive up the Avenue Prince Louis Rwagasore past the American embassy, the embassy continued its stream of cables to Washington chronicling the tragedy, and Washington continued to do nothing. Lest you think that only the Nixon-Kissinger executive could be so devoid of human emotion and mired in its own bureaucracy as to maintain this stony silence in the face of colossal human suffering, consider this priceless glimpse of the racist mentality of our congressional leaders, afforded when Melady's successor, Robert Yost, came up for confirmation on June 23. Senate Foreign Relations Committee chairman J. William Fulbright: "We have been hearing a lot about activities down there. Some of them sound very ominous about the civil strife. Could you tell us a little about that?" Ambassador-designate Robert Yost had been briefed by Melady and by the State Department, but he chose to cover up: "Well, sir, this is something that I am obviously going to have to look into very closely when I get there. There have been a number of reports in the newspapers. . . ." The chairman of the Senate Subcommittee on African Affairs, Gale McGee, then joined in:

> *McGee:* This [violence] is likely to continue with the brutality between them. [In our 1971 visit] we saw people whose legs had been

cut off because they were the tall ones. They simply wanted to equal-
ize the size. . . .
Fulbright: Well, if he [Yost] gets into trouble, he can go down and Mr.
Carter [nominee for Ambassador to Tanzania and also present for confir-
mation] will help out.
McGee: Carter can speak for the tall ones and you can speak for the short
ones and we will have a happy compromise. I have no questions.

Neither did anyone else.

At the end of September, four months and hundreds of thousands
of lives after the genocide began, Washington acted: the new U.S.
ambassador was recalled "to give point to our displeasure." Two
months later, he was sent back to Burundi. What can you do? One of
several courses of action that were open to our government was economic sanctions, what Roger Morris calls "the coffee option." In the
four years preceding the massacre, the United States bought more than
80 percent of the annual Burundi crop, accounting for more than
85 percent of the country's export earnings. The profits on the
$12,000,000 crop do not, of course, go to the three hundred thousand
growers, who are mainly Bahutu; they go to a handful of Batutsi who
control the government, to the coffee board and to the growers' cooperative. One action the State Department could have taken early in June
was an embargo, or even the threat of embargo, on coffee purchases.
We could have vetoed the annual Burundi request to the international
coffee convention for a waiver of quota restrictions on its late crop. Or
the President could have unilaterally embargoed Burundi coffee. Or the
American importer, Folger's, could have been asked informally to forgo
purchasing Burundian coffee voluntarily. Would some such move have
restrained the Micombero regime? "It would have been devastating; an
economic disaster for the government," said a former ambassador to
Burundi. And a former Peace Corps volunteer in Burundi, Jeff Lang,
wrote from Zaire in a letter to the *New York Times:*

> What is so disheartening is that these killings would be so easily stopped.
> Simply publicizing the truth can go a long way, but economic pressure
> cannot fail. The United States holds the key to the situation as the buyer

of 80 percent of Burundi's coffee, its only cash crop. A country so poor as to execute people with hammer blows to the head in order to save ~~bullets certainly couldn't resist any serious economic sanction against it.~~

An indictment of our government as serious as its failure to take the coffee option is its failure, from all indications, even to consider it.

But all of that I learned much later. When David left, I took up our more modest problem: who is John, and where does he come from? While Richard dressed, I tried calling a taxi, only to find the line out of order. Ah-ha! This was the reason the zamu had led us to Elsa's threshold last evening. Returning there to use the phone, I found a handsome young man in tennis garb seated on the divan, fingering his racket; Elsa was dressing and would be out in a minute. I stood in the living room, flooded with sunlight, feeling distinctly uncomfortable and rather like a third wheel. Elsa insisted on driving us to the orphanage herself, and it turned out that one of the housegirls knew the way, more or less.

The Bujumbura orphanage seems to be about the same size as the one in Gitega, though it is much older, quite dilapidated and sparsely furnished. When we arrived, some children were pushing squeegees along the concrete floors, which had recently been hosed. We were led to the supervisor, a pleasant and attractive young woman in Western dress, Imelda Ndikumana. She recognized John from our description and said that she had gone to see him at the hospital when she first came to the orphanage, since the staff had spoken about him.

"His real name is Balthazar," she said, and went to get the orphanage register as we stood dumbfounded. "Balthazar Nsanzerugeze, born 1964. Admitted January 22, 1969. Mentally ill. Father: Ntahonkuriye. Address: Gisagara, Gitega. Mother: deceased."

"My god, Richard. He came here at the age of five. If he was ever in the wild, he was very young."

"Ask her if there's anyone here who was here when John arrived."

There was, and Mme. Imelda brought the aide over and translated our questions into Kirundi. Do you remember Balthazar? Yes. What was he like? Sick. How? You had to feed him by hand, he couldn't chew, he would eat only milk, bread, and bananas. He didn't speak. What else? He was always flapping his hand like this, and he made funny noises. Were you here the day Balthazar arrived? She nods. Who brought him? "I don't know. A nun, I think."

Mme. Imelda believes the White Sisters brought three children to the capital from an orphanage they were closing in Kiganda. One died, one was taken back by his father, and the third one is Balthazar. How did he come to be called John, we asked. Perhaps because no one at the hospital took the trouble to learn his name. If we return after lunch she will take us to visit a nun nearby who was the treasurer at Kiganda and drove the orphanage car; she might have brought Baltha- zar. At that point the directress arrived and, after a rapid exchange in Kirundi, Mme. Imelda suggested that if we were going to ask questions of this sort, we should check with the Ministry of Social Affairs and Work, which we promise to do.

On return to the orphanage, a twelve-year-old who was also named John led us to Mme. Imelda's home. As he instructed our taxi driver, his bearing seemed to carry a certain pride in the responsibility he had been given. He was rather tall and thin, quite a handsome boy with a graceful manner and a shy smile. How different he is from the other John, I thought. How unequally fate has treated the two. Mme. Imelda joined us, and we drove a short way, pulling up in front of a pleasant little house and garden in a residential quarter of Bujumbura. Sister Tonia Roelens seemed to have internalized the tranquillity, simplicity and cheerfulness of her surroundings. Her face was surprisingly free of lines, her skin was quite fair, and all her features seemed poised as she spoke.

"I was actually at the maternity clinic in Kibumbo in 1968, but our order also ran the orphanage in Kiganda. I don't know why people think the White Sisters did. We are the Order of the Immaculate Heart of Mary. You will want to talk to Sister Marie-Jeanne. She was the business manager at Kiganda until 1969 when the orphanage closed. You see, we put a new system into practice that works much better. In Burundi, a child is an orphan if its mother is dead or insane. If the child is younger than five, he can be placed in an orphanage.

FURTHER TESTS

Meanwhile, the father usually remarries, and when the child returns to the family, he is treated like a houseboy. He becomes a Cinderella, is mistreated and often underfed, and develops kwashiorkor. Then he must be sent to a hospital. So we closed the orphanage, and now a father can bring his orphaned child to the mission if he is accompanied by some woman, perhaps a relative, who stays there for two weeks and is taught child care. Then she takes the child away and raises him. And the mission will help her by providing food."

"So," we summarized, "with the orphanage closing in early 1969, Sister Marie-Jeanne might have brought Balthazar from Kiganda to Bujumbura. But where is she now?"

"She's at the mission in Munanira, about halfway between here and Gitega. Here, I'll draw you a map."

VII

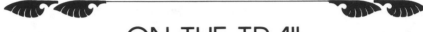

ON THE TRAIL
OF BALTHAZAR

Sister Roelens's map was as clear as could be, but here we are shaking, bouncing, jolting and jostling along some pitted clay road in Bartoli's car. Richard is driving, and we are quite probably lost. Since there are no signs and the last two passers-by did not speak French, there is nowhere to go but ahead.

"After Zarotchintsev, Sister Nestor and Petronille, Madame Imelda and Sister Tonia, after filming, and recording, and examining and X-raying, after five bloody exhausting days, Richard, we're back where we started. What do we know? Nothing."

"We know his identity, Balthazar Nsanzerugeze."

"That hangs by a thread. Some woman, whose name I didn't get, says through a double translation that our description of John matches one Balthazar."

ON THE TRAIL OF BALTHAZAR

"So we go back there with a Polaroid snapshot and question more of the staff; there must be others. We've also pretty much ruled out most of the causes of mental retardation except autism. And we also know that if soldiers caught him in the wild he hadn't been there very long, since he was five when he came to the Bujumbura orphanage, and probably younger when he came to the Kiganda orphanage."

"Assuming he ever went to the Kiganda orphanage, assuming he's Balthazar."

Just before the end of this conversation, we rejoined the paved road in the village of Muramvya. For a few kilometers, we skirted the edge of an elevated plateau screened from the valley below by dense foliage. Soon I spotted a small white signpost that signaled the turnoff for Munanira. We left the highway and bounced onto a dirt byroad that led steeply down the mountainside. A dazzling river of color poured out of a church in the distance, surged up the road toward us, and enveloped the car. There was scarlet and magenta and gold, mandarin, saffron and lemon, emerald and turquoise, iridescent in the bright sunlight. Thousands of colors, hundreds of Africans in their multicolor robes, funneling out of Sunday mass, the foreground of a vast landscape. On the banks of this polychrome river there were verdant fields, but behind there was neither sky nor forest, only space and the very pale purple of mountains that could just be discerned in the distance. I left the car and asked for Sister Marie-Jeanne.

A young boy, perhaps ten years old, took my hand and led me down the road. "Where are you from?"

"From America."

"Welcome to Burundi. What do you think of my country?"

"I like it very much. I am very happy to be here."

"You have seen Burundi. But I will die without seeing America."

We edged our way through the crowd in silence, then, and reached a little cottage beyond the church. Sister Marie-Jeanne, in nun's habit, had about her the same aura of calm, simplicity and orderliness as the room in which we sat. She is Flemish, she explained, and her French is not as fluent as it once was. She was expecting us; earlier, two instructors from the university had come by to inquire about John, and had said that two Americans were on his trail as well. But we were mistaken: she had not been at Kiganda in 1969, although she had often visited. On several visits she saw a retarded child, it seems his name was Pietro, who walked on all fours and was epileptic; he would have convulsions, his eyes would roll up in their sockets, and he would fall unconscious. This didn't sound like John, and the more we described him to Sister Marie-Jeanne, the more it seemed unlikely that John and Pietro were one and the same. Worse yet, since she remembered Pietro, she probably would have remembered John, and we began to think he hadn't been at Kiganda at all. Of course, she said, her memory could be failing her (she appeared to be in her late sixties). I didn't think so.

We had lunch with the sisters of the Munanira mission. We stood while they sang a brief and lovely grace, and then, in the Burundian fashion, we were served soup, chunks of well-done beef, potatoes, beans and salad. Dessert was a cake, a single unfrosted layer of coarse texture. At our urging, Sister Marie-Jeanne and a Filipino sister, Josephine, agreed to go with us to Kiganda to look for the record of seven years ago. They asked only one thing: that we bring them back!

The Kiganda mission is at the end of a dirt washboard road some ten kilometers from the Bujumbura-Gitega highway. The road meanders through the countryside amidst small farms on which bananas, manioc and beans are grown. Native huts are scattered here and there, some singly, some in compounds surrounded by stick fences on which vines of beans are left to dry. The huts are round and plastered with mud except for a small opening perhaps four feet high, and they are covered with thatched roofs. The nuns explained that each hut is usually placed in the middle of a small banana grove; bananas are an important crop since they are used to make beer. As always, there are people everywhere, especially on the road. Women are on their way to market in brightly colored robes, usually with babies on their backs and loads on their heads. A child tending long-horned cattle flogs them off the road and into the bush as we approach. A young man passes on a bicycle. The last stretch is straight uphill, and we come out onto a small plateau with a spectacular view of the valley below. Before us, the

ON THE TRAIL OF BALTHAZAR

Kiganda mission, its arched cloisters of tan brick surrounded by lush gardens filled with multicolored flowers in gorgeous bloom. High above Burundi, an African Shangri-La.

The main building—once an orphanage, now a maternity clinic —is especially majestic. It overlooks a vast valley and many other mountains in the distance. Near the entrance were broad flower beds, exotic blooms in deepest enameled red, in fluffy white, in involuted gold. Enormous lindens cast their shade over the stone staircase between the pillars of the principal arch. The brick arches echo off to either side. And above each is a duplicate arch of purple tile inlaid in the façade. Capping these are several courses of brick, and above it all, a red tile roof. Like the companion church and schoolhouse, the building is ornate yet solid; squat, massive, it bespeaks a wealthy European power come to stay.

We arrive just as a crowd is gathering in the courtyard to see a play; admission is three Burundi francs (about two cents). While Sister Marie-Jeanne goes off in search of the records of the former orphanage, a nun gives us a synopsis of the play. A boy is away from his village studying. While he is gone, his father is killed. He returns and must sell all his cattle to get information about who killed his father. When he knows the name of the murderer, he goes to his uncle to ask his aid in taking revenge. The story reveals a lot about social life in Burundi, the nun explains. It has remained as it traditionally was—rural, organized around the family, patriarchal—despite colonialism and then independence. Traditional beliefs also persist, although two-thirds of the population are at least nominally Christian. Prime among these is the belief in Imana, the creator spirit and intangible life force that inhabits all things. The Murundi believes that natural phenomena and his own fate are the will of Imana, to which one must be fatalistically resigned. Barundi also have a strong spiritual attachment to cattle, which are a medium of exchange and a symbol of wealth.

The father governs all family affairs: he presides over discussions, allocates duties, leads worship, and metes out punishment. The reward for successfully caring for the family is its complete loyalty during his life and propitiation of his spirit after his death. He can expect that vengeance will be sought by his heir if his death is caused by violence, whether by physical attack or by witchcraft. When he dies, his chosen heir, generally the eldest son of the first wife (polygamy is prohibited but practiced), receives legal authority and property. The maternal uncle is particularly respected as a second father. Since independence, the traditional emphasis on family and clan (blood relatives bound through the male line) has been reduced. For one thing, there is not enough land for sons to settle near their father's homestead after marriage. For another, the state recognizes marriage without bride-wealth, so a young man need no longer look to his family to arrange a marriage. Finally, education no longer takes place exclusively within the family compound. About a third of all boys will attend some primary school, usually church run, such as the mission school here at Kiganda.

We never found out whether the Murundi Hamlet achieved his revenge, for Sister Marie-Jeanne signaled to us. We followed her into the mission building, down a cool, immaculate green-tiled corridor. In the rooms to either side, turbaned women with huge bellies lay passive and composed. Sister Marie-Jeanne had found the entry in the register for Balthazar! Admitted September 27, 1966; discharged, September 20, 1968. The rest of the information duplicates that in the register of the Bujumbura orphanage, with one significant exception: Balthazar was born March 14, 1966, not in 1964. Stunned, Richard and I stare at each other. The conclusion was plain: John could not be a feral child, if indeed he is Balthazar Nsanzerugeze. Using the information we had obtained from Mme. Imelda, we traced out a chronology for Balthazar and showed it to the curious nuns.

Born March 14, 1966.
Admitted to Kiganda orphanage September 27, 1966.
Discharged from Kiganda September 20, 1968.
Admitted to Bujumbura orphanage January 22, 1969.
Transferred to insane ward at Prince Regent Charles Clinic June 13, 1972.
Transferred to Gitega orphanage June 1974.

ON THE TRAIL OF BALTHAZAR

Balthazar was six months old when he came to Kiganda, two and a half when he left, just four months older when he entered the Bujumbura orphanage, a little over six when he was taken to the clinic, a little over eight when Sister Nestor took him to Gitega, and a little over ten when we found him there. He has never been out of an institution for more than four months!

It may be difficult to believe, but this discovery left us not crestfallen but exhilarated; the tangle of facts, rumors, people and places was unraveling. The awful possibility that we would never solve the mystery had receded ever so slightly. If John was Balthazar, he was not a feral child. My sole concern at that moment, like an escape artist who has removed five constraints and arrives at the sixth, was to undo the next knot: if John was not feral, what was he?

Was he once a normal child, I asked? Is there anyone still here who worked in the orphanage in those days? Someone who would remember Balthazar? The nuns shook their heads; there were two aides, orphans themselves at that time, who had stayed on. But they are off in the hills with their families, as it is Sunday.

"Can't *you* remember him, Sister Marie-Jeanne?"

"I was in Belgium from 1967 to 1969, perhaps I did see him here before that, but he would have been just one of many infants. I think I might have remembered if he was as abnormal as you say. Also, the boy's family would not have taken him back if he were mentally retarded."

"Perhaps they were obliged to take him back because the orphanage was closing."

"No, the orphanage closed in September 1969, a year after his discharge. And if he were mentally ill, the entry would have noted it."

"Let's put it to the test and find the entry for the sick child you described to us, little Pietro."

"I was curious about that myself and looked him up. Here!" And there was the notation next to his name: *aliéné mental.*

An excited nun interrupted us and held out a hand covered with blood and amniotic fluid. "Shake the hand of the *accoucheuse,* it's good luck." We did so and shared for a moment their pleasure at the safe birth of a new child.

As we rode back toward Gitega we were puzzled and troubled. "Not only can we rule out feral rearing, Richard, we can also rule out a birth defect and any combination of the two—fully three of our four hypotheses, at least tentatively."

"We know that a Balthazar Nsanzerugeze left Kiganda apparently normal, and a child of the same name showed up in Bujumbura four months later. But are we absolutely sure they are the same?"

"Suppose they are, which seems likely. Then how could that child be the same as John? He would have to have developed all his symptoms in only four months! I'm not sure that is possible. What if there is a screw-up in the records, or in the recollections of our informants?"

"We can make the link for sure if we can find his father. We know his surname, Ntahonkuriye, his 'address,' Gisagara, and his province, which is, luckily, Gitega. Pierre should certainly be able to help us find him."

"And if John and Balthazar are the same, our fourth hypothesis looks attractive: The boy was crippled by some childhood disease when he was taken back by the family at two and a half. That would explain why they had to get rid of him again. The father can clarify all that."

When we arrived at the archdiocese it was late afternoon. Father Tuhabonye heard our account with wonderment; so John was not raised by monkeys after all. Unfortunately, Gisagara is not as exact a location as we had hoped. "There are several hills by that name; in fact, the word 'gisagara' means hill, so this man could be living on any hill in the province. But there is one place I know of called that, and it's close. Let's go while it's still light. Oh, Sister Nestor and Petronille have fixed a farewell dinner for you, but I'll send word that we will be late."

Pierre fetched a flashlight and we set out, jolting, jarring, jouncing along a heavily rutted clay road. "I wonder if Bartoli has any idea what's happening to his car," said Richard as it trembled, shook, squealed and vibrated. I thought of the room in Kaeuper's house entirely devoted to spare parts for his motorcycle. It isn't a matter of money; if something breaks, you just cannot get a replacement.

ON THE TRAIL OF BALTHAZAR

"What would we do without Volkswagens?" Pierre grunted, his speech punctuated by thuds. "We have a joke: when the Volkswagens are being loaded on the boat in Germany they say to each other, 'We are being sent as slaves to Africa!' Now this place is called Gisagara," Pierre went on, pointing to the dense brush around us. "Stop the car by those men there."

We stopped, and Pierre made the sign of the cross. The men listened patiently as Pierre went on in Kirundi; I could occasionally make out the name Ntahonkuriye. Then they said a few words. Then Pierre. The conversation was broken by long silences. I held up my pad on which the name had been written, which engendered more Kirundi from Pierre and more laconic replies in chorus by the men.

"These men are puzzled," said Pierre, getting back in the car. "They say, 'If it is written down, it must be so,' but they know everyone on this side of the mountain and they don't know of any such man. The other side of this hill is also Gisagara."

We drove back toward the town and around toward the other side of the mountain. Night had fallen, and I could no longer anticipate the potholes. Surprisingly, I slammed into about as many as during the day, when my every effort was devoted to avoiding them. We stopped another passer-by, who told Pierre that he did know an Ntahonkuriye who lived not far from the road and that he would guide us there. At his cry, some children materialized out of the bush and took up stations to guard the car. Then he led us single file up a deeply rutted footpath. We went upward at a brisk pace through groves of manioc and bananas. The air was warm and moist and laden with that ubiquitous scent redolent of cooked beans. Although there was a full moon, it was screened by the dense vegetation, and one of us would occasionally lose his footing, sending dirt and rocks sliding along the path onto the person behind. The guide was chanting some phrase over and over again in Kirundi.

I managed to speak between breaths: "Pierre, what's he saying?"

"That we come in peace."

"What are you going to tell the father? You can't be direct. He'll be afraid we want to force him to take his child back."

"I thought of that. I mean to tell him that a child is very sick. You are his doctors and must speak to his father."

After about a mile, we stopped. I could make out that we were in front of a compound. There was a fence of sticks covered with dried bean vines and an opening blockaded by branches. We stood around outside this gate and waited in silence. After a few minutes, a young man came and took away the branches one by one. I could see a cleared area, a sort of courtyard, with three large huts thatched with straw. In a little while, another young man came out and invited the four of us to enter the compound. We stood in the clearing and waited. From somewhere we could hear music from a transistor radio. An old woman sat on the ground against the wall of one of the huts looking incuriously around her.

Finally a small man—he couldn't have been more than four and a half feet tall—emerged from the opening beside the woman and approached us. I looked at Richard, whose eyes had also grown wide: the man was the very image of John. Much older, of course, with grey hair, but the small forehead, large eyes, flattened nose with flaring nostrils, and small ears were much the same. The man bowed and held his two hands outward as if to clap. Pierre bowed and placed his two hands touching as if in prayer between those of our host. Then the old man pressed his hands against Pierre's and they exchanged a greeting. There was some talk about the long rainy season. Pierre asked the man aside, outside of the compound, and we followed to monitor the conversation.

"He says his name is indeed Ntahonkuriye, but he has no young child; his children are all grown up and they are there in the compound. Their mother is there, too."

"His first wife died, Pierre. But she had a little boy. Ask him."

"He says he has had no other wife."

"He's lying. An affair then. Ask him."

"He says no. I believe him."

"I don't. I don't believe in coincidences."

"Harlan, this is a Catholic country. If this man were John's father, he must have had a mistress while he had a wife who gave him several sons. It's unlikely. And I'm a priest; I don't think he would lie to me. I explained that the child is sick. The man is deeply moved and wants to help. I grant you Ntahonkuriye is an uncommon name, but it is not unique."

"He looks like him, Pierre."

"He is not the boy's father. Trust me, these are my people."

It seemed impossible! The old man volunteered that he did know of someone not far who adopted his brother's retarded child for a while and then relinquished the boy to an orphanage. The man's name was not Ntahonkuriye, but perhaps John's father had died and this man sheltered the boy for the four months between Kiganda and Bujumbura. We set out again, and made our way by flashlight over another mile or so of footpaths to another compound. Again we stood before the gate of branches; again our guide called out that we came in peace; again the branches were removed and a man emerged from one of the huts; again, greetings and pleasantries about the weather were exchanged. Again, Father Tuhabonye asked about the boy John. This family had adopted a retarded child whose name was Martin. The man went in search of his nephew's baptismal card, explaining that the boy was now in the orphanage at Bujumbura, but he had not had word of him in a long time. The card showed Martin to be only seven; we copied the details and promised to inquire after the boy on return to the capital and to send word.

The wrong Ntahonkuriye on the wrong Gisagara! Even Richard seemed subdued.

"How would you go about locating someone here in the province if you only knew his last name," I asked Pierre on the way back. "Are there marriage records, census lists, anything like that?"

"Baptismal records, of course, but you don't know the boy's age for certain; the records are kept in two different locations, and one is far from here."

"Are all the children baptized?"

"Most, but by no means all."

"Tell us where the baptismal records are kept; we'll be there when they open tomorrow morning."

THE WILD BOY OF BURUNDI

It was now about eight-thirty in the evening, and we had another vital matter to deal with. In order to complete John's medical workup we would have to take him to Nairobi, and in order to do that we needed the permission and the company of Dr. Deogratias Barakamfitiye, head of the Gitega clinic and one of Burundi's leading physicians. Bartoli and Tuhabonye had told us that the decision would be entirely his. We had to wait a bit at Barakamfitiye's house in town. Unlike the European doctors, he was working on Sunday.

Deo is a handsome, commanding man in his mid-thirties, but he has only been a physician since 1972. Over a round of the inevitable beer, I told him in French the story of John as we understood it so far, carefully including the necessity of obtaining further tests and the impossibility of doing them in Burundi.

We knew that even a wealthy Burundian would not have the means to travel, and I made clear that our grant would be able to provide round-trip plane fare plus the same per diem that we were receiving—$40. Deo was a sphinx.

I recalled Ethel Albert writing, "the total, glacial silence of a perfectly immobile Mututsi who has chosen not to speak has to be experienced to be appreciated." According to her, this is an effective rhetorical technique that can withstand every known technique of provocation. We seemed to have found the key, however, because Deo finally asked, "Will our accommodations there be the same?"

"Of course."

"You two will be flying on to Paris after one night, and the boy will return here?"

"Yes."

"Would there be any reason why I could not stay another few days in Nairobi?"

We had anticipated this question while we were thinking about how to approach Deo.

"The per diem is only possible for the two days that we will be there, but you may of course stay on and return whenever you wish."

Deo was careful not to show any excitement, but after an impassive silence he said, "I can't think of anything to say against this plan."

ON THE TRAIL OF BALTHAZAR

So it was settled. We arranged to rendezvous with him and Bartoli in Bujumbura tomorrow to get the necessary passports.

At nine-thirty we returned to the orphanage for the dinner Nestor and Petronille had fixed for us, which we enjoyed with Pierre. We decided to use that occasion to tell him of the gift of $500 we wanted to give to the orphanage. It was surely unfair to Tuhabonye, but we wanted to be as certain as possible that the gift would be used for the orphans whom it was our intention to help; therefore, we contrived to tell him about it in front of Nestor and Petronille. His reaction surprised us by being wholly neutral—neither pleased nor disappointed. As the Batutsi say: something revealed is something given away.

Petronille gave us two small Burundi drums as farewell gifts, and we gave her an American Indian necklace. After dinner we went to our cells for a brief planning session—then to bed at eleven-thirty.

MONDAY, MAY 31—MUGERA

When we left the orphanage in the morning, I noticed a sign posted on the main door:

John, Monkey Boy
Visiting hours 9–5
Donation 50 francs

I was reminded of a Burundi proverb I had heard some time during the past few weeks: A man who tells no lies cannot feed his children.

Our search for John's baptismal record began at the Gitega parish with the help of a Belgian priest, Father LeCoq. He was the first white person we had seen in Gitega. Father LeCoq was excited by Balthazar's name. "In Kirundi, Nsanzerugeze means 'I find hate near' or—a better translation—'I find death is near.' A child might be named this because of an unusual circumstance surrounding his birth, and therefore he might not have the same surname as the others in his family."

The three of us scanned through the baptismal registers for 1964 to 1966. We had to cast a wide net, since we were uncertain of John's age and the entries were in the order of the child's baptismal date, not the date of his birth. Small crosses inked in next to a name meant that the child had died. On every page of eleven names, three or four had crosses. After an hour we had collectively looked at more than three thousand names, exclaiming each time we found a Balthazar (there were three) and particularly when I found an Ntahonkuriye, but his name was Joseph and none of the other details matched.

"It is possible that he wasn't registered," Father LeCoq explained. "Perhaps his mother died in childbirth and the father never brought the boy to the parish."

"Could he be registered anywhere else in Gitega?"

"Yes, there is another parish in Mugera serving the more remote side of the mountain. It's about twenty-five kilometers from here. I'll draw you a map."

As usual, we were soon lost on a rutted jeep track in the depths of the countryside. At a fork we would shout "Mugera? Mugera?" to passers-by. Some would point to the left, some to the right, and others back the way we had come. We proceeded by consensus until we found an elderly gentleman who knew French and was going very close to Mugera. When we let him off, I asked if I could take his picture with the Nikon. He struck a dignified pose while I took a Polaroid shot to give him by way of thanks. We watched puzzlement, surprise, then utter astonishment pass over his face as the image materialized from the snapshot. "Is this magic?" he asked, and we assured him that as far as we knew, it was.

The Mugera mission was the most remote we visited. Like the others, it was perched on a lofty summit overlooking a valley, at the end of a steeply ascending path that meandered through groves, farms, cattle, sheep and people of all ages. There were four buildings in beige brick gathered around lush tropical gardens. Numerous workmen were tending various flower beds and patches of vegetables. We sat at a long, hand-hewn table in the refectory hall, drank coffee and chatted in French with a very old priest, perhaps eighty, who had been there forty years.

"Americans! I taught myself to read English, but I cannot tell how the words are pronounced from the way they are written. You write

ON THE TRAIL OF BALTHAZAR

'Jerusalem' and say 'Babylon.' Mugera is the oldest mission in the country. Founded by the White Fathers in 1899. I'm not counting the one at Rummonge that lasted only a year; the missionaries there were accused of working for Arab slave traders and were murdered."

Later, in Paris, I found a diary recounting the first days of the Mugera mission, written by one of the three Belgian priests sent there by the bishop with this charge:

> We must penetrate to the very heart of this country, if we want to become firmly implanted. If we receive the good auspices of the King Mwezi, a rather autocratic king as word has it, the subordinate chiefs cannot harm us. Go then into the center of Urundi and firmly implant yourselves there. They say the country is densely populated where the two great rivers of the country meet, Ruyubu and Ruvyironza, the sources of the Nile. This is the center of Urundi; this is where you must settle. May God grant you his blessings!

On February 11, 1899, the fathers crossed the Ruvyironza, "not without difficulty," and camped on a spur to the south of the mountain of Mugera. "I have often heard that the mountain is sacred," one of the fathers wrote, "and no one may settle there. This is not true: there is a fairly dense population on the sides of the mountain. If people do not settle at the top, it is because life would be impossible there as a result of the rocks and poor soil." Eight days later, armed deputies arrived from the royal court, leading a bull. "What are you doing here? This mountain belongs to the king. We are instructed to tell you to leave. And quickly, on pain of death." The fathers ignored the warning and refused the gift of the bull. Six days later, another set of ambassadors and another warning unheeded. Then began a war of nerves. One day, warriors swarmed over Gisagara mountain facing Mugera, raising a great clamor, beating their drums, trumpeting their horns, but never crossing the Ruvyironza. The fathers knelt and prayed the whole time.

Next the natives tried casting a spell on the fathers: they sent a bewitched bull into their midst; they scattered magic powder around the camp. The fathers decided to send an envoy to the German military camp at Muramvya, which was headquarters for a campaign against the mwezi (the grandfather of Mwambutsa IV) who had refused to accept German sovereignty. One native bearer after another was slaughtered en route to the camp. Finally one got through and returned with three German soldiers and a promise of a visit by the commandant as soon as the present campaign was over. This happened soon after, and following the promised visit, the local chiefs, who had formerly been hostile, or at best indifferent, came forward to welcome the missionaries. More than forty of the royal clan, including three sons of the king and ten ganwa, brought the fathers gifts.

In the ensuing months and years, the Germans waged a desultory war against the mwezi. Once he narrowly escaped with his life by changing his royal garments for the loincloth of a servant. When the German soldiers saw the decoy, they fell upon him and took his life. The king was left with few illusions about his fate if he should be caught and he sent a delegation to the mission at Mugera to plead with the fathers to intercede with the Germans in his behalf: *"Zimya umuliro! Zimya umuliro* [put out the fire]!" he begged.

In the end, the mwezi was captured. The treaty of Kiganda, signed in 1903, required him to pay 424 cattle in reparations, to allow caravans to travel freely about the country, and never again to threaten the mission at Mugera. And so it remained to this day.

"Do you think we could look in your registers?" we asked the old priest.

"They are registering the children now," he said, and led us out across the sunlit garden to a small building where there was a queue of some thirty native women, each holding a baby in her arms, each wearing a brightly colored robe, each waiting quietly. The queue led through the doorway to an old wooden table where, quill in hand, a still older scribe, with grey hair and spectacles, was bowed over the register entering a child's name in flowing script. After an exchange in Kirundi, registers were distributed and our search for Balthazar began anew. Suddenly, Richard found it:

> No. 86851. March 21, 1966. Balthazar _____. Born March 17, 1966. Father, Ildephons Ntahonkuriye (Gisagara). Mother, Sindaharaye (Kishuhu). Mother died, March 26, 1966.

ON THE TRAIL OF BALTHAZAR

With this information, the scribe could find the family card, which showed that Balthazar's parents were married September 17, 1953, that he has two brothers and three sisters, the oldest now twenty-two, and that his father died in 1967. I noted that the last names were added in different colors of ink. Abbé Roger explained that children were not usually given a last name until a year or two after birth, when they had a reasonable chance of surviving. All the siblings had the father's surname except Balthazar. His mother died nine days after he was born, so now we understood why he had been given the ominous name of Nsanzerugeze. Our search for his father was over, and Pierre was right about the old man in the hut in Gisagara. We had traced Balthazar back to his beginnings.

But we lacked proof that Balthazar is John. After some debate, we decided that it would be best not to track down the brothers and sisters. They lived at a distance, and their hut, according to our abbé, could only be reached on foot. Further, the oldest was only eight at the time Balthazar was born and might not be able to tell us much of his early health and his mother's illness. So we accepted the priest's offer to send for them at a later date and question them in our behalf.

Since Kiganda is on our way back to Bujumbura, we decided to try and find either of the aides who worked there when Balthazar was a baby. Maybe one of them will remember some abnormal behavior, a description, something we can tag to John. We have the Polaroid snapshots of John, and they might identify him as Balthazar.

The drive was not long and it did not take long to find one of the two aides, Anna, an attractive young woman of about twenty-five.

"Be certain," I emphasized to the Flemish nun who agreed to help us, "Be certain that you do not give her any clues about the identity of the child we are interested in."

"She was not here yesterday, and we have said nothing to her today." The nun interrogated Anna in Kirundi as skillfully as any counsel for the defense, beginning with the snapshot. "Do you recognize this child?"

"I think so, but it was a long time ago and he was very little then."
"Who is he?"
"Balthazar. What has become of him?"

"He is sick and these two doctors are trying to help. Do you remember what year he was brought to Kiganda?"

"He was about two when he left, maybe three. That was a year before the orphanage closed in '69. So he must have come in '66; he was just a baby when he arrived."

"Do you remember who brought him?"

"Some woman, but I don't think it was his mother. An aunt perhaps."

"What was he like?"

"An ordinary baby. Like all the rest."

"Nothing special about the way he looked or played or ate?"

"No."

"Did he talk?"

"A little. Like every other baby."

"Were any of the children mentally disturbed?"

"There was one. Pietro. He had fits."

Anna was taken to a side room while the second aide, Hélène, was sent for. There was no mistaking her laugh of recognition when she saw the picture. She added only that she had been present when a man came to take him away from the orphanage. She didn't know whether it was his father or a relative.

On the ride back to Bujumbura we summarized the case:

John's mother died a few days after he was born, probably as a result of childbirth. He was placed in the Kiganda orphanage at six months of age, apparently a healthy child but an orphan, since his mother was dead. While he was in the orphanage his father died. When he was about two years old, a relative came to claim him. He appeared normal at the time he left the orphanage because both Anna and Hélène remember him that way and also because his relatives would not have reclaimed him if he were evidently retarded. He was with a family for four months, during which time his symptoms appeared. Then he was given up by the family, probably taken back to Kiganda, and a nun did the service of taking him to the orphanage in Bujumbura, because of their plan to close. From that day to the present, he has spent his life in institutions, so we can rule out the theory that John spent any extended time in the wild. His symptoms must be due to disease; their late onset and the tests we were able to conduct so far implicated autism more than any other illness.

But this possibility raised new questions; autism is quite rare and only recently the subject of medical research. No one knows its cause. Heredity? Complications during childbirth? The result of infectious diseases that give rise to encephalitis? And the most important question: can autism begin at age thirty months or go undetected until then? Our informants reported that John was normal until that age. What we would learn in Nairobi could provide conclusive evidence for autism, or on the other hand, could point toward some other childhood disease.

At three we arrived at the Prince Regent Charles Clinic. We saw M. Laurent, a nurse and Zarotchintsev. Predictably, another Russian shortly joined us. We asked if there were any records for one Balthazar Nsanzerugeze. This proved to be a single blue file card with a few notes: "Admitted, June 13, 1972. Diagnosis: psychosis (malaria)." The boy had a high fever that day, no doubt the reason for his being brought there from the orphanage. The record says he was given quinine. Then, eight months later, there was a urine test recorded—negative. There was no further information, no discharge, but we know that he spent three years there living among the psychotics before being taken to his present home in Gitega. We recounted our findings to Zarotchintsev and said our farewell, as we had with Pierre and Nestor.

"So, there are no monkeys in the story?" mused Zarotchintsev.

"No, none," I replied.

"I wonder if there are any in Burundi. I've never seen one."

Oral literature is at the top of the aesthetic scale, Albert had written of the Barundi. There, literal truth gives way to practicality and aesthetic values. The emphasis in conversation is on elegance of composition, figures of speech, interpolation of stories and proverbs—themselves unclassifiable as true or false. For me there was a delicious irony in hearing Zarotchintsev contrast the bald truth about monkeys with the legend of John: I had drawn a similar contrast between fact and fiction when I was in the Soviet Union a decade ago, and I had received a lecture from a high-ranking official on the necessity of placing the social good achieved by an account of events over the literal accuracy of the account. One thing was becoming increasingly clear: an account of what happened always has several functions. There is no such thing as "the truth, the whole truth and nothing but the truth" unless we understand "truth" to refer not only to particular environmental events but also to the social context in which they occurred.

A SECRET
LONGING

From Richard's diary

A distraught ambassador and an alarming cable from the State Department awaited us at the embassy the following morning. We gathered from the message that our telegram to Boston on arriving at Gitega a week before had never been received, and that our failure to get blood samples onto the Bujumbura-Brussels flight, as planned, was also misinterpreted.

FM SECSTATE WASHDC
TO AMEMBASSY BUJUMBURA NIACT IMMEDIATE 3359
SUBJECT: WHEREABOUTS OF PROFESSOR HARLAN LANE
1. DIRECTOR, NORTHEAST UNIVERSITY PUBLIC RELATIONS DEPARTMENT, CONTACTED DEPARTMENT LAST WEEK REGARDING WHEREABOUTS OF PROFESSOR LANE, UNESCO-ASSOCIATED PSYCHOLOGIST, WHO WAS SCHEDULED

THE WILD BOY OF BURUNDI

ARRIVE BUJUMBURA FROM BRUSSELS MAY 23. LANE PROMISED TOM SPRAGUE, NORTHEAST UNIVERSITY, HE WOULD CONFIRM ARRIVAL TO EMBASSY. HE ALSO PROMISED SEND CERTAIN SPECIMENS BACK TO BRUSSELS BY PLANE SCHEDULED ARRIVE YESTERDAY. LACK OF INFORMATION OR SPECIMENS HAS HIGHLY ALARMED UNIVERSITY, SINCE LANE IS APPARENTLY ACCUSTOMED TO FOLLOW INSTRUCTIONS METICULOUSLY.

2. LANE IS INVESTIGATING ALLEGED CASE OF CHILD BROUGHT UP BY ANIMALS, REPORTED BY JOHANNESBURG PRESS. STORY IS SAID TO AROUSE GREAT INTEREST IN SCIENTIFIC CIRCLES. ACCORDING SPRAGUE, LANE WAS IN CONTACT WITH TWO BURUNDI BISHOPS WHO PROMISED MEET AND ASSIST HIM AT AIRPORT. CHILD IS SUPPOSEDLY LOCATED IN KITEGA.

3. TO AVERT THREATENED PRESS RELEASE ALLEGING DISAPPEARANCE IN BURUNDI, APPRECIATE IF EMBASSY WOULD: A) FIND OUT FROM AUTHORITIES WHETHER LANE EVER ARRIVED IN BURUNDI; B) CONTACT LANE TO ENSURE HE IS ALL RIGHT; C) FIND OUT IF AND WHEN HE PLANS SEND PROMISED SPECIMENS.

4. PLEASE AT LEAST CONFIRM BY OOB WHETHER LANE ACTUALLY ARRIVED IN BUJUMBURA. SISCO

Whether the ambassador was more annoyed at the unnecessary fuss or at the fact that he had not been alerted during the night as the heading NIACT IMMEDIATE requires, I couldn't tell. He sent off a sharply worded reassurance and received this reply.

SUBJECT: LANE/PILLARD VISIT
REF: (A) STATE 134263; (B) BUJUMBURA 445
1. DEPARTMENT APOLOGIZES FOR INCONVENIENCE AND CONFUSION CAUSED BY REFTEL A WHICH, AS A RESULT OF SPRAGUE'S CALL DURING LONG HOLIDAY WEEKEND, WAS DRAFTED AND APPROVED BY PERSONS UNAWARE OF THE BACKGROUND OF LANE/PILLARD MISSION. NORTHEAST UNIVERSITY PUBLIC RELATIONS OFFICIAL WITH WHOM DEPARTMENT NORMALLY DEALS ON MATTERS RELATING TO LANE/PILLAR MISSION ALSO SENDS HER APOLOGIES TO EMBASSY AND PROFESSORS FOR SPRAGUE'S PRECIPITOUS ACTION WHICH GENERATED REFTEL A.

2. ACCORDING TO UNIVERSITY, LANE/SPRAGUE TELEGRAM (PER REFTEL B) NOT RECEIVED. THEREFORE, WOULD APPRECIATE RECEIVING CONFIRMATION OF LANE/PILLARD ITINERARY FOR RETURN TO U.S. HAS TEAM DETERMINED THAT JOHN IS BONAFIDE FERAL CHILD? IN VIEW OF MEDIA INTEREST, WOULD TEAM BE AGREEABLE TO HOLDING PRESS CONFERENCE UPON ARRIVAL BOSTON? KISSINGER

A SECRET LONGING

At our request, the ambassador was kind enough to cable the American embassy in Nairobi:

SUBJECT: ASSISTANCE REQUEST FOR U.S. PROFESSORS LAND AND PILLARD

1. DRS. LANE AND PILLARD, UNESCO ASSOCIATED PSYCHOLOGIST AND PSY-CHIATRIST, HAVE JUST CONCLUDED ONE WEEK OF INTENSIVE LOCAL BACK-GROUND INVESTIGATION AND PHYSICAL EXAMINATION OF BURUNDIAN CHILD WHO WAS WIDELY REPORTED IN U.S. PRESS TO HAVE LIVED WITH MONKEYS IN JUNGLE. PROFESSORS HAVE DISCREDITED THESE STORIES, BUT NEED NONETHELESS TO COMPLETE THEIR EXHAUSTIVE PHYSICAL EXAMINA-TION IN NAIROBI TO FULLY DETERMINE NATURE AND EXTENT OF CHILD'S MENTAL RETARDEDNESS.

2. BOTH PROFESSORS, A BURUNDIAN DOCTOR, AND THE 10 YEAR OLD CHILD, BALTHAZAR NSANZERUGEZE, PLAN TO ARRIVE NAIROBI ON AFTERNOON OF JUNE 2 VIA QC 060. THEY HAVE REQUESTED NAIROBI'S ASSISTANCE IN ARRANGING ADMITTANCE OF CHILD INTO HOSPITAL (KENYATTA HOSPITAL WAS SUGGESTED TO THEM) ON EVENING, JUNE 2. ON FOLLOWING DAY, JUNE 3, THEY WOULD LIKE TO HAVE THE CHILD ADMINISTERED AN ELECTROEN-CEPHALOGRAM WHICH WOULD ALSO REQUIRE HIS ANESTHETIZATION. THEY THEMSELVES WILL CONDUCT SEVERAL ADDITIONAL TESTS.

3. AMEMBASSY BUJUMBURA AND DEPARTMENT HAVE FULLY SUPPORTED THESE SERIOUS AND TALENTED PROFESSIONALS DURING THEIR STAY IN BUJUMBURA, AND WOULD APPRECIATE AND ENCOURAGE WHATEVER SUP-PORT AMEMBASSY NAIROBI CAN EXTEND TO THEM. WE MUCH REGRET THE UNAVOIDABLE LATENESS OF THIS REQUEST AND HOPE THAT IT WILL NOT CAUSE YOU TOO MUCH DISCOMFORT.

4. WE HAVE SUGGESTED THAT PROFESSORS CONTACT DR. BEAHLER ON THEIR ARRIVAL IN NAIROBI.

MARK

Dr. Barakamfitiye joined us at the embassy at nine-thirty sharp, and we set out to see the minister of public health. Deo has no passport and before we leave tomorrow must obtain one for himself and what-ever documents may be needed for John-Balthazar. Kaeuper had ex-plained to us that the minister of health and the minister of passports don't get along; he predicted that we would spend two weeks mired in Burundi red tape. We bet him tonight's dinner that we'd have it done in four hours.

Dr. Joseph Nindorera welcomed us warmly and thanked us for our efforts. We know that John's true identity is Balthazar Nsanzerugeze and we have ruled out the possibility that he was ever raised by monkeys, we explained, or ever spent any time in the wild. We believe he is suffering from a childhood disease, perhaps one known as infantile autism, for which there is no medical and little psychological treatment possible, considering how extensively damaged he is. His failure to develop any language or significant learned behavior by the age of ten suggests that he will always be profoundly retarded and require custodial care. Before finally adopting this conclusion, we would like to complete our medical tests in Nairobi with the aid of sophisticated facilities and a pediatrician. The minister immediately agreed and made two calls. One was to expedite visas for Deo and the boy; the other was to summon two psychologists at the University of Burundi who, as we had heard, had also been tracking down the history of John.

The psychologists appeared within minutes. It is hard to judge a Murundi's age, but they looked like graduate students. With a wry smile the minister rebuked them gently: "You fellows have been working on this for months, and these two Americans figure it out in a couple of days." We all felt uncomfortable. "At least," one of them ventured, "it turns out to have nothing to do with the 'events' of 1972." "Events" was the delicate word everyone used to refer to the genocide.

Cyrille Barancira and Nicephore Ndimurukundi were open, pleasant and eager to learn about psychology in the United States, knowledge which we were as eager to share over lunch at the Paguidas Hotel. Too bad we hadn't time to visit the university, or become better acquainted with these young professors, who, we sensed, might have been willing to give us some insight into the political and social life of the country. We exchanged addresses and promised to send them some psychology journals from the States.

After lunch, we paid a visit to the Assistance Sociale, the Ministry of Social Welfare, as we had promised Mme. Imelda we would. A dismal building surrounded a dirt courtyard where dozens of horribly maimed people formed a grotesque queue. In a tiny dark office we found Mme. Leocadie Niyondiku, who had directed the orphanage in 1969 when Balthazar arrived. We had hardly begun our explanation to her when she recoiled in terror. "You must speak to the director of welfare; I can tell you nothing . . . please."

At the director's office: "Could we speak to Mme. B., who directed the orphanage here in 1972, when Balthazar was taken to the clinic?" The pudgy director stared at the piece of glass on top of his desk and spoke to us softly. "You are mistaken; a man directed the orphanage in that year." Could we speak with him? "He is gone now." Gone where? Perhaps we could . . . "He is just gone." We guessed the terrible truth and left.

Four-thirty P.M. Since our last visit to the orphanage, Mme. Imelda had found an aide, a man of middle age, on the staff for many years. He spoke only Kirundi but identified our photograph of John and described his symptoms—the fanning, chattering, head-banging. Balthazar had always been that way, the aide assured us, ever since the day he arrived in 1969. He was, however, otherwise healthy and did not have a fever until 1972, when he was taken to the clinic.

For dinner, we collected on the bet with Kaeuper.

WEDNESDAY, JUNE 2—BUJUMBURA/NAIROBI
From Richard's diary

At the airport, Deo, Sister Nestor, Petronille and John, on time to the minute, are waiting for us with Bartoli and a reporter from the national radio station. He tapes a brief interview that concludes on this note: "Thus ends the legend of John, the Jungle Boy." I kept feeling that there was something "foreign" about this young reporter and then I recognized it: he is the first fat person I have seen in this country.

While we were waiting for the plane we asked Bartoli about the $60,000 of American relief that Kaeuper claimed were merely waiting for a contractor's estimate. Why had it taken the Burundi government so long to act? Bartoli rolled his eyes. "We are well aware of the sixty thousand dollars, my friends. The estimate is ready. Only we will wait a few more weeks because we have made a request to Catholic relief, and it will be better to hear from them before we accept the U.S. money." Bartoli said that he had tried to explain this to Kaeuper at lunch, but neither his English nor Kaeuper's French was adequate for communication. What madness allows our foreign service officers to be stationed in a country where they do not even know the language of government, not to mention (oh, sublime ambition!) the language of the people.

Not many people have traveled Air Zaire, but jets are the same everywhere. An uneventful two-hour flight with a stopover in Entebbe. We took turns managing John. Debarking in Nairobi, John immediately drew a crowd of people who recognized him from newspaper accounts and an almost life-sized picture on the front page of *Africa Trends*. Momentarily I worry that the crowd may become a mob, but a getaway cab is at hand and a call to the American embassy confirms that the Jomo Kenyatta Hospital and an American pediatrician, Dr. Alan Cross, are expecting us. I check us into a hotel near the hospital; Harlan and Deo get John settled into the pediatric ward, and we join Alan Cross for dinner at an Italian restaurant in downtown Nairobi.

Whatever is wrong with American health care, you would expect that a few doctors like Alan could make it right. A young pediatrician just finishing his training, he wanted to see Africa and brought his wife and child for a two-year stay. He seems thoroughly American, with a direct manner, enormous energy, a great interest in our little patient, and a serious appetite for Italian food.

We returned to examine John directly after dinner and found a rather tired, unusually calm little boy having diarrhea all over his crib. Cross confirmed that there were no serious physical abnormalities and with his ophthalmoscope got a rather good look at John's retinas. There is some dark pigment, but it's a normal variation, and I too was convinced of this after managing a brief look.

Alan is not optimistic about arranging an electroencephalogram on short notice. It usually takes two weeks to schedule, a couple of days even in an emergency. We spot the chance for another bet; we will have the EEG by two in the afternoon and then Alan will take us to Nairobi's famous game park. A deal!

As late as it was, we were all too keyed up to quit. Alan agreed to show us his ward and the hospital. The Kenyatta Hospital is the

A SECRET LONGING

central referral facility for most of Kenya, so the pediatric ward was filled with interesting cases. Here is a child with Burkitt's lymphoma, a rare and fatal disease; here a congenital malformation of the heart called tetralogy of Fallot; over here a rare and as yet undiagnosed case of anemia; here a child who had begun life as a hermaphrodite, with both penis and vagina—the penis had been surgically changed to a clitoris. As always, our doctor's instinct for the exotic case contends with our human distress at the sight of ill and suffering children. In another ward we see infants in bassinets under high-intensity fluorescent lights—a recent treatment for jaundice of the newborn. We pass through the emergency ward, crowded with mothers sitting up all night to attend their sick little ones. Several children are connected to a cardiac monitor, which signals automatically when the patient's heartbeat becomes irregular. In the X-ray room, a giant automatic processor takes in an exposed X-ray, develops, fixes, and dries the film, and spits it out in six minutes.

Cross is complaining that the hospital has nothing compared to medical centers in the States while Deo is bug-eyed at the wealth of equipment. It's midnight and we are to be back here at eight tomorrow to get things cooking.

THURSDAY, JUNE 3—NAIROBI
From Richard's diary

The Hotel Pan-Afrique is Europeanized enough to put the day's paper on your tray with coffee. I awoke to find we were celebrities. The page 2 headline read:

CHILD, ADOPTED BY WILD APES, NOW UNDERGOING HOSPITAL TESTS
Nairobi, June 3 (UPI)—A young boy who was raised by wild monkeys in Central Africa has been admitted to a Kenya hospital for a battery of brain tests and observation. . . .

I dressed quickly, tossed the paper under my arm, and headed for the lobby, where I found Harlan and Deo. We hailed a cab and were at the hospital in five minutes.

THE WILD BOY OF BURUNDI

Our strategy for expediting the examination was for Deo to approach his African counterpart, Dr. Martin Odouri, head of pediatrics. When he did this, emphasizing his government's interest in seeing the tests completed, the pediatrician called the EEG technician and booked an appointment for noon. But the technician wanted the approval of the hospital administrator, who was less ready to grant it. Of course, if we were prepared to pay something for these services, a contribution to the hospital development fund . . . We immediately agree, though concerned that our money is running out. The administrator calls the technician and tells him to charge us something, though it is difficult to say how much, because medical care is free to all citizens of Kenya. On return to the EEG lab, the technician has found the correct charge: three hundred Kenya shillings (forty dollars), which I count out on the spot and he pockets. We think it wisest not to ask for a receipt.

Barakamfitiye has left to make contact with the Burundi consul while Harlan and I watch as the pediatric residents draw blood and spinal fluid from John. It takes three of them to hold our patient, who is struggling and screaming. Every cry makes the veins in his neck stand out like cords. This helps the process, as Dr. Odihambro guides his needle into the external jugular vein, a good source of blood when the arm veins are too small. I notice myself joining the cool detachment of the residents. It's something we all learn starting with the long days and nights of patient care in medical school and internship. You have to do procedures that hurt people, and you have to do them swiftly if you are going to get any sleep. You don't face the crusty chief of service next morning at seven-thirty rounds with an excuse like "I tried twice to do a spinal tap, but I couldn't stick that crying child another time!" Unthinkable! So you learn to objectify people and their pain. The mercy for John is that the team is efficient. In minutes they are done, and we go off to spin the blood, freeze the serum and spinal fluid, and make a few slides.

For lunch we have a nondescript bun and tea in the hospital cafeteria and serve John a cocktail: twenty-five milligrams of chlorpromazine and one gram of chloral hydrate. Presently he is sleeping lightly and we slip a frame on his head bearing a dozen electrodes, and paste each one in place. During the hook-up, reporters from a Kenya newspaper, the *Nation,* arrive to take pictures and to interview us. I am opposed on the grounds of good form, and besides, Harlan had promised the networks before leaving that we would not leak the story. Deo also disapproves of the pictures and calls his consul for advice. But the hospital administrator urges us to cooperate. A compromise is reached: since John is on Alan's ward, Alan will make a statement to the press in the waiting room; no pictures. He leaves with Harlan, Deo and the reporters (Harlan will give Deo a running translation of the statement) while the technician and I proceed with the EEG. The slow regular traces testify that John is asleep most of the time, and I try mightily to rouse him by shouting in his ear, clapping and the like so we can get both waking and sleeping records of brain activity. After a half-hour or so, we are finished; our fifty yards of paper record the electrical activity at some thirty positions on John's scalp. The technician offers to arrange an appointment for us with the hospital neurologist, who will read the tracings (at a glance, they look abnormal). We go off with John to radiology to arrange another set of X-rays while he is sedated. The radiologist agrees to join us in an hour to review all the findings.

With John back in the ward and all the physicians assembled, Harlan made an opening statement.

"First, I want to thank all the hospital staff here for their extraordinarily helpful and rapid response. Balthazar Nsanzerugeze is a mentally retarded ten-year-old male from Burundi whose parents are deceased. He has many of the behavioral symptoms of infantile autism. Piecing together his case history, we have been able to establish that his mother died in childbirth, that the onset of his symptoms was between thirty and thirty-four months of age, and that, contrary to popular belief, he has never spent any significant period of time in the wilds. We hope that you can help us answer the following questions: Is there any evidence of organic brain damage? Is there any evidence that would support or disconfirm that diagnosis of autism? Is there evidence of some other syndrome of retardation or of a childhood disease that might cause this symptom picture? What are Balthazar's acute medical problems? Finally, your thoughts on diagnosis, treatment and prognosis would be appreciated. Can we start with the X-rays?"

"They show no abnormalities," the radiologist replied. "The frontal swelling due to self-abuse is not accompanied by a thickening of the skull. The bone and jaw X-rays confirm that he is about ten years old. There are no bony structure abnormalities to account for his toe gait. Sorry I can't be more helpful."

"How about the EEGs?"

"We've got something there. The tracing is abnormal. Against a background of well-organized moderate-voltage activity, ten to eleven cycles per second, the recordings show brief runs of high-voltage focal slowing—in the right posterior temporal region and in the left occipital region, spreading on one occasion to the left posterior temporal region. The record suggests diffuse encephalopathy."

"Alan?"

"Most of the blood tests are normal except for an elevated white cell count and a very elevated eosinophil count, suggesting a chronic allergic reaction and possibly an acute infection as well. His stool contains eggs of the trichinae parasite. We could worm him, but it's hardly worth subjecting him to that procedure, since he will be reinfected in a week. The cerebrospinal fluid is clear and the pressure is normal. The urine is normal. The things that stand out from the admissions workup are lack of speech but funny mouth noises, fanning, toe gait and distended belly."

"So, to return to my questions, there is evidence of organic brain damage, no evidence of any childhood disease other than autism, and Balthazar's only acute problem is worms: the diagnosis would appear to be autism. He has all these clinical features: symptoms beginning before age three; underreactive to sound; repetitive hand-flapping; fearful of sudden changes in illumination; reduced eye movement and eye contact; disinterest in games; inability to form peer relationships; no language; toe-walking; body rocking; head-banging; maternal illness; abnormal EEG. Quite a list! Further, he is mentally retarded but without an "island of excellence," an anomalously developed talent like art or music, often found with autistic children. An even more disturbing fact: no trace of these symptoms until he was thirty months old.

One of the residents on Cross' ward spoke up: "No problem there. You've got two kinds of autism. In the first, mothers report that their children behave strangely shortly after birth. In the second, though, the parents report relatively normal development up to about two years of age. The child may even start learning to talk, and then unaccountably he relapses into the autistic state. Perhaps a third of all autistic children fit into this late-onset category, and they end up doing no better than the early-onset cases."

"So Balthazar could have been normal when he left the orphanage at two and a half and then become symptomatic shortly after," Harlan said.

"He might have contracted the disease in any of several ways," I broke in. "The first is birth injury of some kind. Studies show that perinatal complications are more common in autistic individuals than in control groups. Second, there are the childhood diseases—mumps, measles or even malaria—that cause encephalitis and leave permanent brain damage. I couldn't cite hard figures, but various case studies report an autistic syndrome after a serious childhood disease."

"That's my own preference here," the neurologist said. "Measles is the most likely cause of diffuse encephalitis with permanent sequelae. The EEG is consistent with diffuse encephalopathy of remote origin manifested by mental deficiency and autistic behavior."

There was a third possible cause—defective chromosomes or genes. The first factor to consider is chromosomes: children with mongolism or Down's syndrome have an extra number 21 that leads to their particular physical appearance and mental retardation. But the chromosomes of autistic children appear to be normal. Defects in the genes carried by the chromosomes, genes that are responsible for the production of enzymes required for metabolism, may also be implicated. But these defects are much harder to study. The fundamental evidence for genetic transmission is to observe that parents, siblings, or ideally, identical twins, have the disease more often than random persons in the population. Suppose, for example, that a gene carried in the X or sex chromosome causes autism, as is the case with hemophilia. Since four times as many males as females are autistic, genetic theory tells us that, if the disease were sex-linked, 1 in every 4 males would have it! Fortunately, the frequency is more like 1 in 2,500. Then suppose the mutant gene is carried by one of the other chromosomes. If only one copy is sufficient to produce the trait, the gene is said to be dominant. Certain kinds of dwarfism are produced in this way. But with a dominant gene, the trait appears in both sexes equally, in generation after generation, and about half the children of an autistic parent would also be autistic. This just isn't the case. Suppose the gene causing autism were, like that causing PKU, recessive—that is, two copies of the same mutant gene are required before the individual expresses the trait. In that case, the parents of an autistic child may appear completely normal (since each has only one copy of the gene), autistic children should more often be related to each other (since consanguineous marriage will bring the copies together), and about 25 percent of the children in a family should be affected. Autism fails the last two tests: the recurrence rate for siblings is about 2 percent.

Another possibility is that several mutant genes are required at the same time to produce the trait. If three recessive genes had to be present, the recurrence rate among brothers and sisters would be 1.6 percent, quite close to the 2 percent reported; however, that wouldn't explain why males are affected more often than females. Of course, autism might not be a genetic disorder at all, but one reason that idea won't go away is this: identical twins both have the disease more often than fraternal twins, though the number of cases is small. Balthazar was not a twin, and the odds that one of his brothers or sisters is autistic would be very small.

A study by Hauser, DeLong, and Rosman suggests that damage to the temporal lobe is the proximal cause of autism. They injected air into the spinal canal to temporarily replace the cerebrospinal fluid, then X-rayed the brain. Air filling the ventricles normally occupied by fluid showed up on the X-rays, and it turned out that in many of their cases, the left ventricle was larger than the right, suggesting that the left temporal lobe was for some reason shrunken or diseased. That's significant because the left temporal lobe is, for most people, the part of the brain used to process language.

Alan Cross proffered Balthazar's prognosis. "He is profoundly retarded and will require twenty-four-hour institutional care all his life. Also, he has a good chance of developing seizures. It's interesting that autism and mental retardation don't always go together. Some autistics are normal or even have exceptional skill, such as in music, but of course even the bright ones don't use language or emotional communication much. On the other hand, I have seen severely retarded youngsters with no more verbal ability than Balthazar who nevertheless smiled and made good social contact with adults. With this condition, however, there really isn't any treatment. What can you do?"

As the conference broke up, I reflected for a minute on John's future. In the States he would be in an institution such as the Fernald School, where the stress of working is so great that some wards have an almost complete turnover of personnel every few months. Who would know John or learn to care about him? At the Gitega orphanage he has Sister Nestor and Petronille, who adore him, and a stable environment. Given that there is nothing we can offer in the way of treatment, I feel more than satisfied with the care he will get in his native land.

On return to the ward, we found what seemed like half the employees of the hospital crowded into that small space trying to get a look at John. We were told that some TV cameramen had just left, having taken a picture of him eating bananas. Cross was furious and threw everyone out. As he began to speak with a reporter from the *Nation,* another from *Der Spiegel* arrived. Then the nurse told him he had an overseas phone call, so I took on the reporters. "It was WBZ on the phone from Boston," Alan explained on returning a half-hour later. "They wanted a live interview. I told some newscaster there was no truth to the original rumors, so he asked me where I was from, how I liked Africa, what were the jungles like, did I have enough to eat and so on. Then the Voice of Kenya called, and I agreed to a live interview tonight."

At that point a CBS film crew arrived with a reporter from the

Standard, and Alan exploded. While we barred the entrance to the ward, he went off to find the hospital administrator, who, as it turned out, was at that moment receiving a telephone reprimand from the minister of information, who wanted to know why he hadn't been informed. Harlan went off to help draft a press release. Deo was scandalized by the press coverage; I suspect he feared it would make him look like a circus master and not a doctor. Harlan agreed, and said he felt that all Deo's optimism, enthusiasm and joy at seeing Nairobi and the Kenyatta Hospital had been smothered. Deo is disappointed in each of us. Some introduction to the West! Later, however, he seemed to have recovered. We apologized for the press but he shrugged it off: "It's their job, isn't it?"

The examination and conference were finished, and it was exactly three o'clock. We were a bit behind for our bet, but Alan was delighted to show the three of us Nairobi's most famous tourist attraction. The National Game Park is a savannah beginning within sight of the city and extending several hundred miles toward the Serengeti. Big game animals wander freely here, and it is we, the visitors, who must stay in a cage—in this case, Alan's small car, which the game warden instructed us never to leave. Deo's reserve dissolved into amazement as three giraffes, one of them a baby only six feet tall, bobbed toward the car. There is no game in Burundi, and of course there are no zoos, so we had the pleasure of affording Deo his first sight of what Africa is famous for. Alan was good at spotting the animals, and with his field glasses we saw about thirty species, including one worried baboon perched on top of a road sign scanning the endless horizon for his pack.

It was not easy for us to say goodbye to Deo; it meant a lot to us to have met him; we promised that somewhere, somehow, we would meet again. As for Alan, it was simpler. Deo would arrange an invitation for him to visit and consult on pediatric care in Burundi; and we would see Alan in a year's time when he returned to the United States. Lastly, there was Balthazar. But at that moment he didn't enter our minds. If you think that is strange or hardhearted, you must try to understand the difference between caring for a friend and caring for a patient. Of course, one can become the other, but two basically different postures are called for—one subjective, the other objective. Deo and Alan had become our friends and we were sorry to separate; it left us feeling incomplete. Balthazar was our patient and our puzzle; we had done what we could for and with him; we felt complete.

A few hours later we checked in at Nairobi airport with nine cases. We had left our toys and medical supplies behind. But we were richer by one styrofoam case of frozen blood, one set of X-rays and EEG tracings, two native drums and a few souvenirs, the solution to a mystery, and countless ineradicable memories.

"We should work on a press release," I told Harlan. It was two in the morning, I couldn't sleep, and we were somewhere over Africa en route to Paris. "I'm sure everyone will start by assuming that the story of John the monkey boy is a hoax."

"You know, we really have little to criticize Barritt for. The government restricted his stay to three days and his itinerary to Bujumbura and Gitega; he spoke neither French nor Kirundi. So he learned what he could. His story was sensationalized a bit, but he didn't make it up."

"We also have the story in the Swedish newspaper *Kvällsposten* that Henri showed us in Paris. That was written in December before Barritt ever got to Burundi. All right, but what about Pierre and Nestor? How would you rebut the theory that they made it up? Maybe they saw an opportunity to attract attention to the orphanage and get some help?"

"They wouldn't fabricate a story when the details are so easy to check. We found out in a few minutes that John was in the clinic when the legend had him in the woods. For all they knew, his real father could have come forward and exploded the theory."

"And Pierre would never have been so curious and so helpful if he had something to hide. I agree, Harlan, they clearly didn't make it up, but I'm willing to believe they fed the story when they saw an opportunity to attract attention to the orphanage and maybe get some help."

"You can hardly fault them for that if it's true; what they want is powdered milk for the kids, for Christ's sake. But John is not just

Balthazar misunderstood. He has, so to speak, his own reality. We now know what gave rise to Balthazar—autism. Before we can say that our search is really through, we have to understand what gave rise to John."

"Well, John is a character in a legend. It developed like all good legends, from the bottom up. People liked the story, they repeated it, embellished it, added dates, details. The conditions for developing a myth were all there: John is a very strange child, unaccountable and anonymous because Balthazar had lost his identity moving from institution to institution with almost no records. The oral tradition of Burundi society is central in this story. Except for the Tutsi elite, most of the population cannot read; the only newspaper is a mimeo sheet and it's in French; all education is in French; and after the massacre every Muhutu who could do more than write his name was dead. This means people are only informed by word of mouth, and there you have the climate for the development of rumor and legend."

"True enough. And of course, Richard, he does act a bit like a monkey: fans himself, chatters, devours bananas. So you have a small boy of obscure origins with monkeylike behavior who turns up in the midst of a people with an oral tradition. They 'explain' him as well as they can. But the reasons for the legend must be more fundamental. Do the 'events' of '72 fit in here?"

"All the versions of the myth connect John with the so-called events. We know that at that time, May and June 1972, he was in the orphanage and then the clinic. We also know that the director of the orphanage and probably some of the staff were murdered at that time. That doesn't explain why they sent John to the clinic—after all, he had a high fever and I'll buy that as the reason they took him there—but perhaps it explains why he wasn't brought back; the orphanage was in administrative chaos. However, I was thinking about something different. Perhaps John is a symbol to the Burundi people, a symbol of the massacre victims. Here's an unknown kid, alone and lost. The atrocities have resulted in his becoming like an animal. It reminds me of one of the theories the psychologists, Cyrille and Nicephore, discussed with us, that perhaps the 'emotional perturbation' made him mute. He is unable to speak after the horrors he has witnessed. We know, of course, that this isn't true, but it may be a way for Batutsi and Bahutu to talk about the tragedy indirectly, and for at least some Batutsi—they're the ones who are caring for him—to indicate that they want to heal the country's sickness."

"It's reasonable for a psychiatrist to sound neo-Freudian, but you are more sanguine about the Batutsi than I am. Even if that is a motive for their interest, it isn't a motive for ours. Why have wild boys had this fascination for us in all times and places? Why did the press swarm over us? Why, nearly two centuries ago, did Victor attract the same kind of publicity—articles in every newspaper, long discourses in scholarly books?"

"We've been over some of that. Victor was the impossible experiment. We could learn from him how we are like and unlike animals. Wild men fascinate us because they help us to understand ourselves. And it impresses me that that was true in Victor's day. Darwin wasn't born yet and *On the Origin of Species* wasn't published until 1859, but even in Itard's time, men seem to have been wondering about our relationship to animals; they seem to have intuited that our life in a 'society' is somehow derived from animal life in the 'wild.' "

"That will explain the interest in real wild men, Richard, but not the legends. What lies behind this very intellectual picture of our interest in real wild men and our quite visceral fascination with the legendary ones? We need an explanation for both. I remember a quote from Franck Tinland's wonderful book about wild men; he says: 'Mute and hairy, wild men join hands with a long train of fantastic beings who, in the depths of the forests, waver between bestiality and divinity.' Or something like that. The problem, anyway, is to explain the fascination of Victor but also that of John; of Selkirk, a real sailor isolated on an island, but also that of Robinson Crusoe, the fictional character he inspired; of Kroeber's real Indian, Ishi, but also of Voltaire's fictional one; of Kasper Hauser, Amala and Kamala, but also Mowgli and Tarzan. To say nothing of all the wild men that have crowded art, theater and heraldry from antiquity through the Middle Ages to the Renaissance—from Romulus and Remus to Rousseau's noble savage. Like all legends, wild men must exist to meet some human need."

THE WILD BOY OF BURUNDI

"Now you're sounding neo-Freudian, and for a student of Skinner surprisingly so."

"Well, on this point at least the two camps agree: in fiction we can do what we dare not do in real life. Skinner frankly admits that he has Frazier say for him in *Walden Two* what he himself dare not say in William James Hall. And there, it seems to me, lies the source of our fascination with wild men. It is an attempt at escape, escape from the fetters of society. In contemplating a Victor or a Tarzan, we let our minds roam where we ourselves cannot; we live vicariously what we dare not and cannot live in reality."

"It's easy to see how that applies to Itard's fascination with Victor. What you say about him in your book makes him sound emotionally inhibited, even for the standards of the day."

"Do you know what Itard said about Victor's growing sexuality? He wanted to reveal to him—that was his word, reveal—the secret of his restlessness and the aim of his desires. But if I did, Itard asks, musn't I fear that Victor would satisfy this want as publicly as all others and commit acts of revolting indecency? By which he meant delicious indecency. He writes: What if this child of nature were to rape everyone? He means: I am partly a child of nature; what if I were to rape everyone? He went to his grave a bachelor and recluse, by the way, without having revealed to Victor the secret of the boy's restlessness or to himself the secret of his own."

"What you're saying then, Harlan, is that the wild boy legend, like a dream, allows us to escape from the surveillance of society, our superego, and to act out our sexual impulses. I swear, Harvard will take back your degree! Isn't there also something more general, a desire to escape from the trammels of civilization and back into the state of nature? Let our instinctual feelings be expressed as they are felt? Recapture serene, tranquil moments of days gone by when we, too, communed with nature? Remember the letters people sent us before we left: what right have you to tear this child from his life in the forest? That sort of thing—as if people believed, or fantasized, a better life in the forests of Burundi than in their hometowns. What a comment on the human condition if a man can come forward and honestly say: I would trade all that society has achieved, all the knowledge that has been passed down to me from my forebears, reaching back to antiquity; I would trade my daily comforts, my leisure activities, my family and friends, my work, my hobbies, literature, art, music, in a word, my way of life; I would trade all that to be free in the jungle. Probably no one would so baldly make that trade, but certainly all of us feel that in the bargain with with Nature, we have given up something."

"Remember, Richard, what people want is vicarious escape, not real escape. We are attracted *and* repelled by wild men at the same time. Seduced by the child of nature who is in touch with the way the universe was before society, but likewise revolted by this grotesque, partially formed image of ourselves; proud of the distance we have traveled from a foul, mute, convulsive urchin; frightened that the veneer of civilization is just that and can be peeled off in one swoop; nostalgic for the time when we, too, could be ourselves with no before thoughts or afterthoughts, irritated by this quasi-human reminder of our humanity. The legend of the wild boy holds an eternal fascination for us because it is the scene of an eternal battle between instinct and reason, between I and we, in which neither force can emerge victorious because our humanity requires both. Perhaps these life forces are, finally, the masculinity and femininity in each of us. Symbolically, man is virile, strong, biologically capable, woman the civilizing influence. I'm not saying the symbolism is accurate. I'm just saying that men are more readily cast in the feral role than women; but the desire to rehabilitate the feral child has a more feminine connotation. Each of us, of course, embraces both symbols and both sets of desires. Hence, our fascination with these shadowy creatures who speak to both sides of our personality; hence, the legend."

"So we're returning home with solutions to mysteries. Who is John? Why did a legend grow up around him? Who is Balthazar? What's wrong with him? But we're not returning with a feral child. Aren't you disappointed just a little?"

"I can't say I'm not; the opportunity for science would have been magnificent, and after studying Victor . . . How about you?"

"My interest was naturally more in the psychiatric and medical issues. For me, the reality was as rich as the legend. But I agree, it would have been the find of the century."

"If Skinner calls me again one day about another John, Balthazar or Victor, do you want to hear about it? Would you do this all again?"

"Yes, wouldn't you?"

"Yes."

INDEX

INDEX

INDEX

‡ 185 ‡

INDEX

mutism, 10, 11, 13, 49, 54, 58, 64, 65, 73–74, 75, 78, 112, 176–77, 179
Mwambutsa IV, Mwami, 69, 133–34, 156

Napier, J. R. and P. H., 40
Napoleon I, 56
Nation (newspaper), 170, 173
National Assembly (France), 137
National Broadcasting Company (NBC), 35
National Game Park (Nairobi), 174
National Guard (Finland), 63
National Institute of Child Health and Human Development, 26
National Institute of Mental Health, 26
National Institution for Deaf-Mutes, 49, 50, 51, 54, 60
Ndikumana, Imelda, 9, 139–40, 142, 146, 164, 165
Ndimurukundi, Nicephore, 164, 176–77
Ndizeye, Prince Charles, 135
Nelson, Avi, 35, 39–40
neurology, 22, 171
Newsweek (magazine), 39
New York Times, The, 52, 138
Nile River, 81, 91, 133, 155
Nindorera, Dr. Joseph, 163–64
Nixon, Richard, 26, 137
Niyondiku, Mme. Leocadie, 164–65
Noigenegene, Elizabeth, 9, 125
Northeastern Press Bureau, 25
Northeastern University, 29, 34, 41, 161, 162
Nova (television series), 18, 21, 25, 28, 32
Ntahonkuriye, Ildephons, 139, 148, 156
Ntare V, Mwami, 69, 135
Ntuyahaga, Father Michel, 38
Nyanza Lac, Burundi, 9
Nyerere, Julius, 136

Nzisabira, Sister Nestor, 98, 99, 119, 120, 142, 148, 153, 159, 165, 173, 175

Odouri, Dr. Martin, 168
Ollivier, Vince, 35, 81
On the Origin of Species (Darwin), 177
Onigman, Marc, 36
ophthalmology, 126, 127
Order of the Immaculate Heart of Mary, 140
Organization of African Unity, 136
Orphélinat Officiel de Bujumbura, 9
otology, 60

Pagé, Father, 38, 81–85
Paguidas Hotel, 29, 164
paleontology, 49
Peace Corps, 7, 13, 88, 138
pediatricians and pediatrics, 21, 22, 77–78, 164, 166–68, 174
Peter (wild boy), 80
Peter of Hanover, 72, 73
philosophy, 49, 52, 53, 62
photodocumentation, 18–21, 24–25, 28, 109, 119, 124, 142
phrenology, 56
physiology, 22, 58, 114
physiotherapy, 78
Pietro (disturbed child), 144, 147, 158
Pillard, Elija, 34, 36
Pinel, Philippe, 49, 50, 52, 54–57, 58, 90, 106
Poizner, Howard, 38
polygamy, 146
preparations, 15, 16–44
 arranging photodocumentation, 18–21, 24–25, 28
 consultation with experts, 21–25, 34–37
 dealing with reporters, 34–35, 37–40, 44
 finding an associate, 17

INDEX

INDEX

INDEX

Harlan Lane, author of the highly acclaimed *Wild Boy of Aveyron*, received his B.A. and M.A. from Columbia University in 1958, and his Ph.D. under B. F. Skinner at Harvard University in 1960. For some years he was a professor at the University of Michigan, where he was also the director of the Center for Research on Language and Language Behavior. He was then visiting professor at the Sorbonne for five years and received his Doctorat d'État in linguistics. In 1973 he returned to the United States and was visiting professor at the department of linguistics at the University of California in San Diego for a year and a half. He is now chairman of the psychology department at Northeastern University, where he also directs a research program sponsored by the National Science Foundation, on the American Sign Language of the Deaf.

Richard Pillard grew up in Ohio and graduated from Antioch College and the University of Rochester School of Medicine. He trained in psychiatry at University Hospital in Boston, then received a Research Scientist Development Award from the National Institute of Mental Health to pursue research in psychopharmacology. He has published a number of articles on psychotropic drugs and marijuana. He also does research on the development of sexual orientation.

Dr. Pillard is currently associate professor of psychiatry at Boston University School of Medicine, medical advisor of the Homophile Community Health Service, a Fellow of the American Psychiatric Association and the Royal Society of Health, and a member of the Society for Psychophysiological Research and other scientific organizations.

He has three daughters, is divorced, and is an accomplished pastry chef.